FOR ORGANS, PIANOS & ELECTRONIC KEYBOARDS

E-Z PLAY TODAY

119

BLUES

ISBN 978-1-4950-0789-7

HAL•LEONARD®
CORPORATION

7777 W. BLUEMOUND RD. P.O. BOX 13819 MILWAUKEE, WI 53213

Visit Hal Leonard Online at
www.halleonard.com

Ain't No Sunshine

Registration 8
Rhythm: 8-Beat or Blues

Words and Music by
Bill Withers

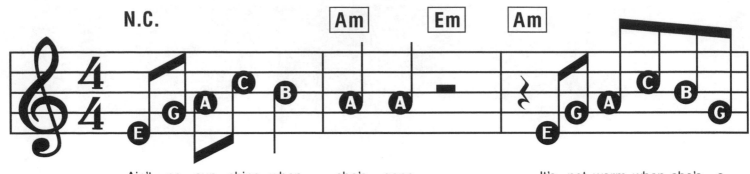

Ain't no sun-shine when she's gone. It's not warm when she's a-

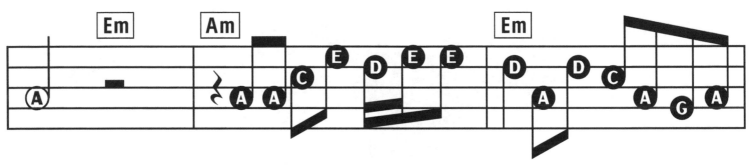

way. Ain't no sun-shine when she's gone, _____ and she's al-ways gone too

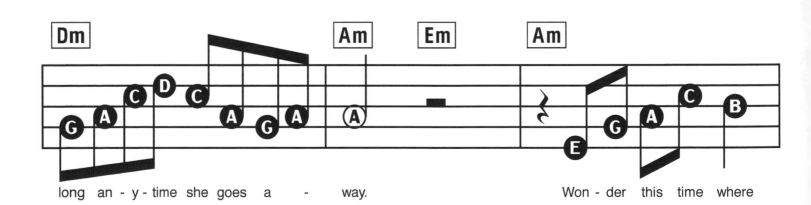

long an-y-time she goes a - way. Won-der this time where

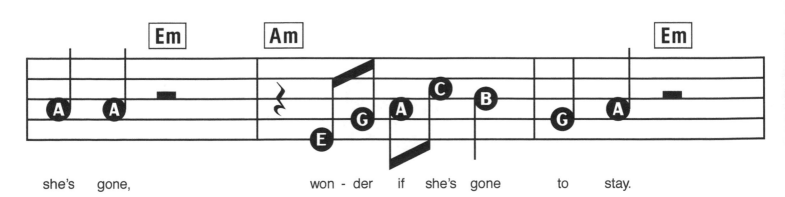

she's gone, won-der if she's gone to stay.

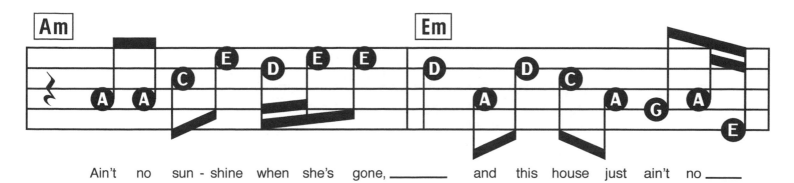

Ain't no sun - shine when she's gone, _____ and this house just ain't no _____

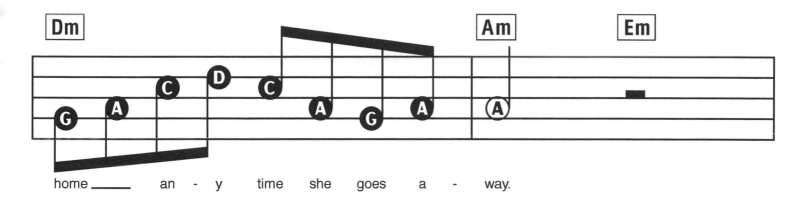

home _____ an - y time she goes a - way.

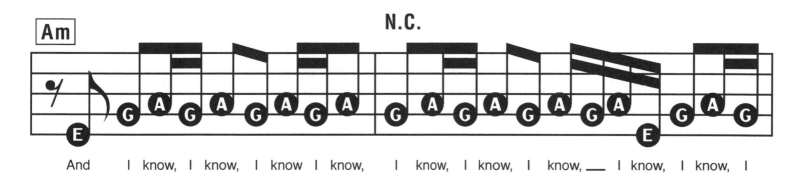

N.C.

And I know, I know, I know I know, I know, I know, I know, ___ I know, I know, I

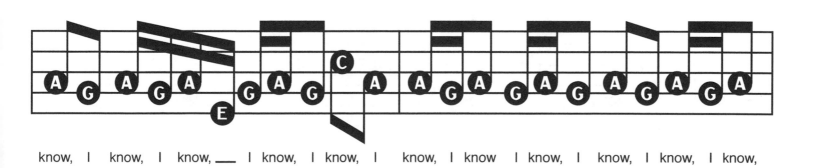

know, I know, I know, ___ I know, I know, I know, I know I know, I know, I know, I know,

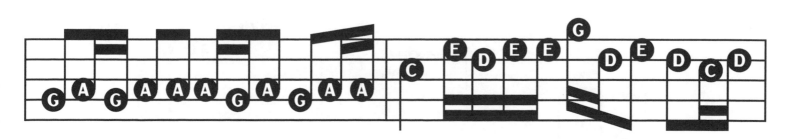

I know, I know, I know I know, I know, I know, hey, I ought to leave the young thing a - lone, _

3

Flip, Flop and Fly

Registration 2
Rhythm: Shuffle or Rock

Words and Music by Charles Calhoun
and Lou Willie Turner

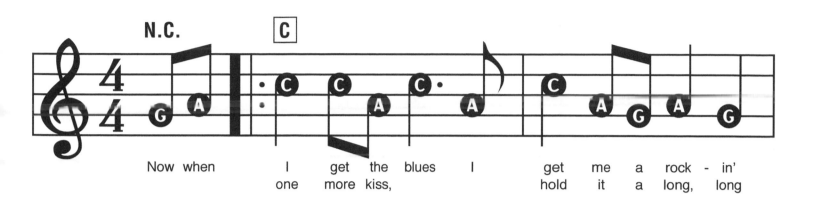

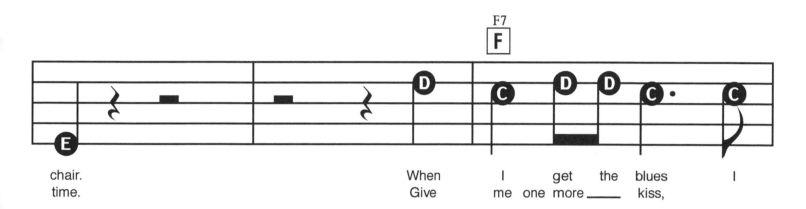

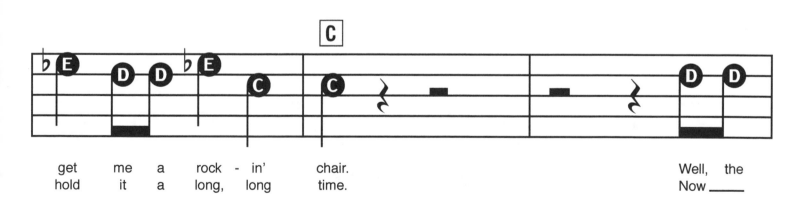

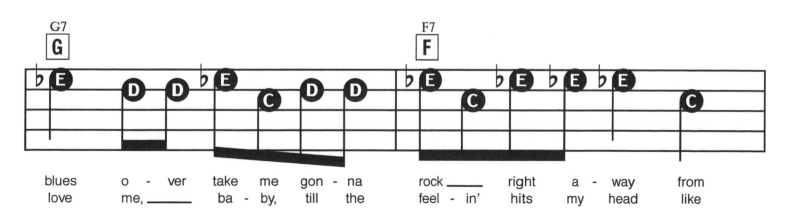

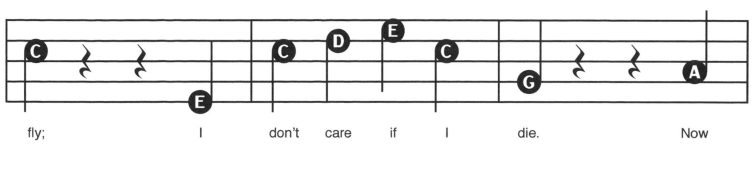

fly;   I   don't   care   if   I   die.   Now

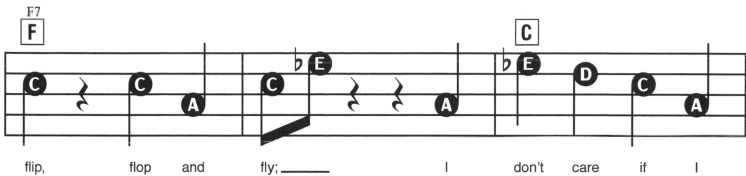

flip,   flop   and   fly; _____   I   don't   care   if   I

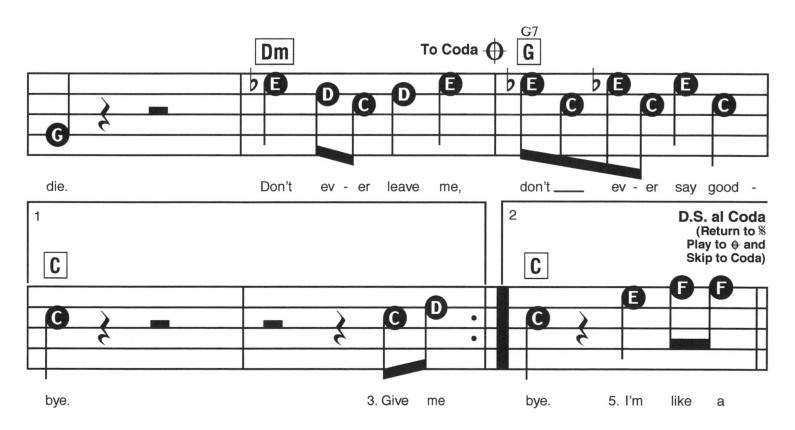

die.   Don't   ev - er   leave   me,   don't ____ ev - er   say   good -

bye.   3. Give   me   bye.   5. I'm   like   a

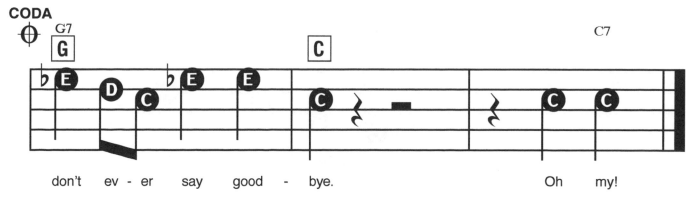

don't   ev - er   say   good - bye.   Oh   my!

At Last
from ORCHESTRA WIVES

Registration 3
Rhythm: Ballad or Swing

Lyric by Mack Gordon
Music by Harry Warren

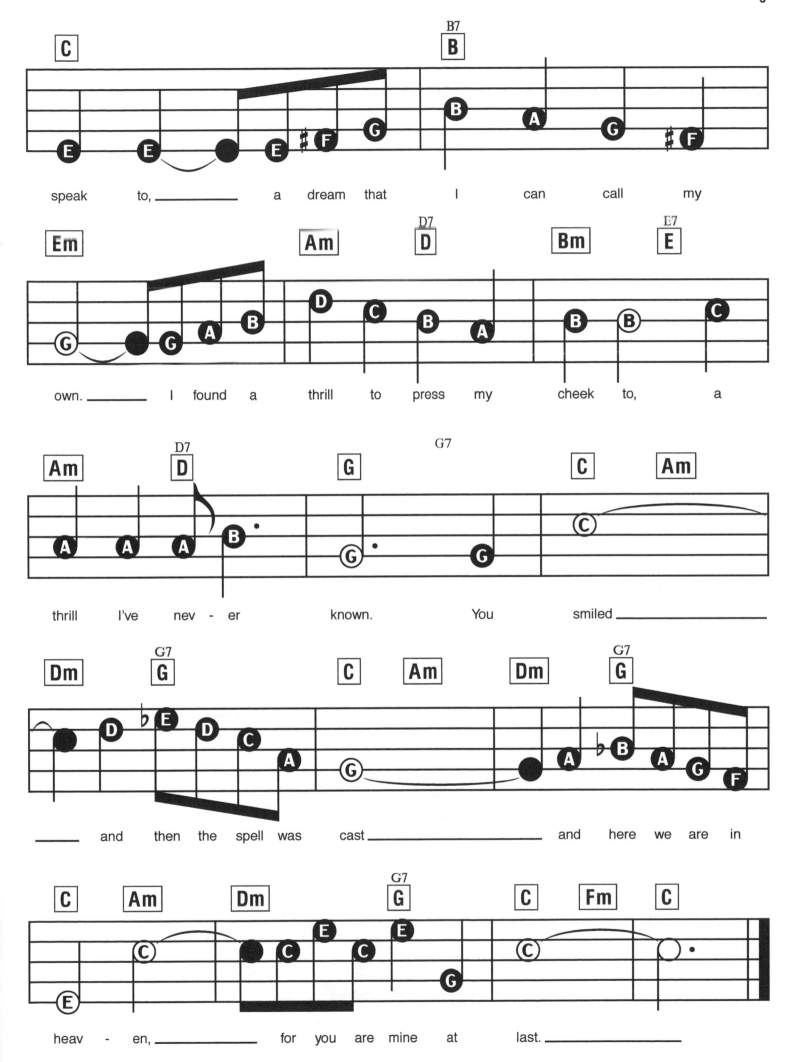

Basin Street Blues

Registration 1
Rhythm: Swing or Fox Trot

Words and Music by
Spencer Williams

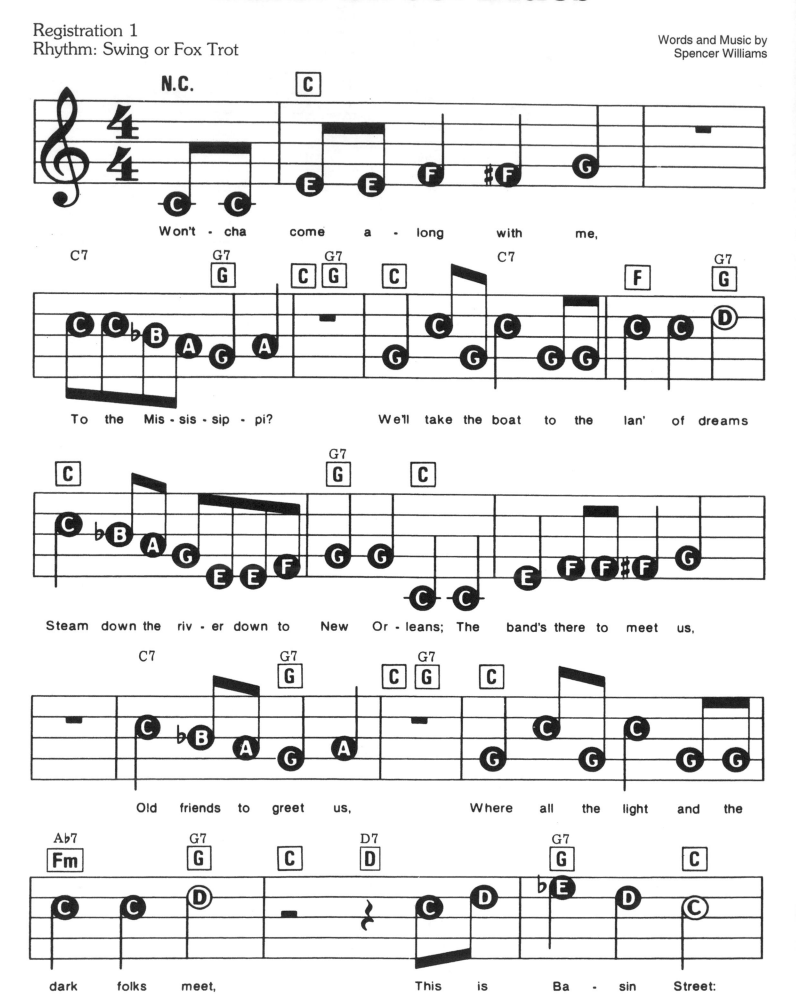

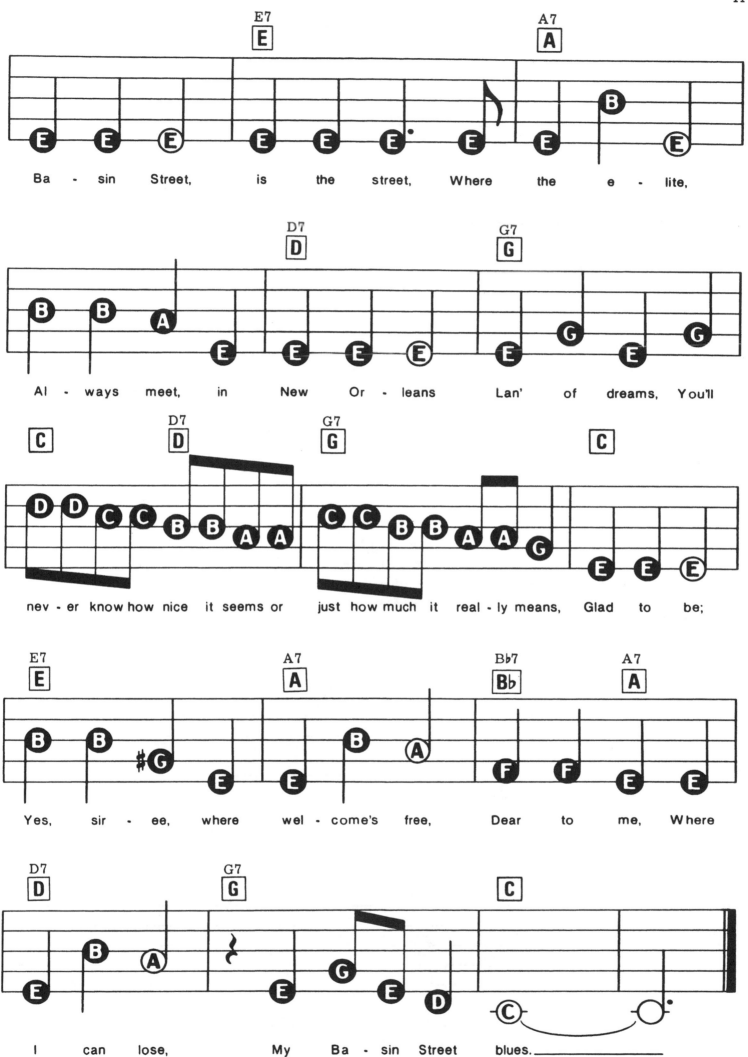

Caldonia
(What Makes Your Big Head So Hard?)

Registration 1
Rhythm: Swing

Words and Music by
Fleecie Moore

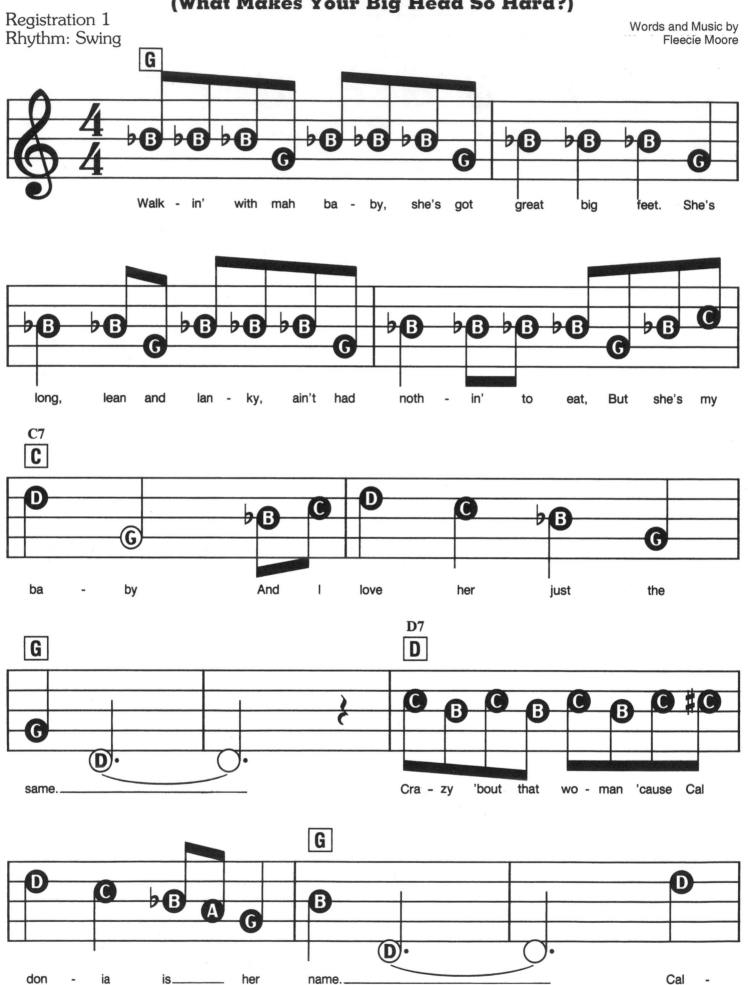

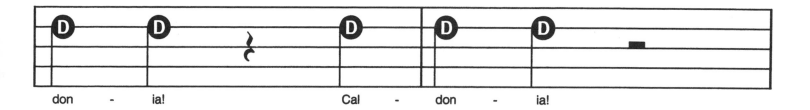

don - ia! Cal - don - ia!

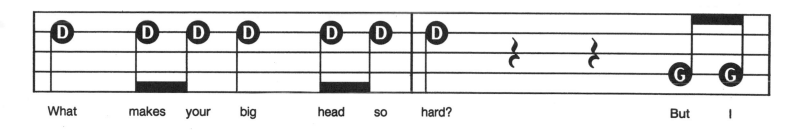

What makes your big head so hard? But I

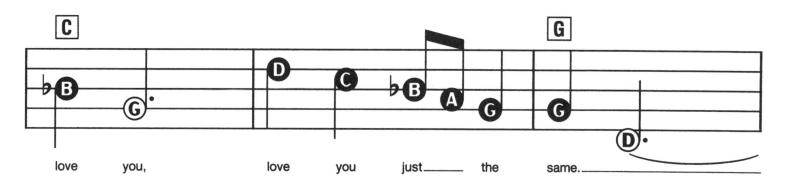

love you, love you just____ the same.____

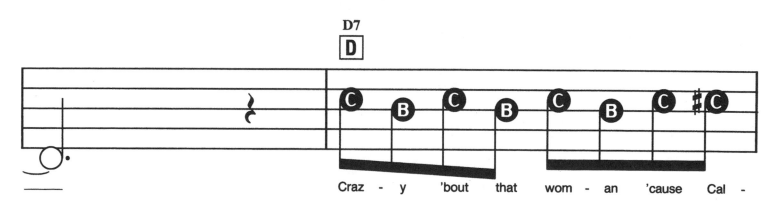

____ Craz - y 'bout that wom - an 'cause Cal -

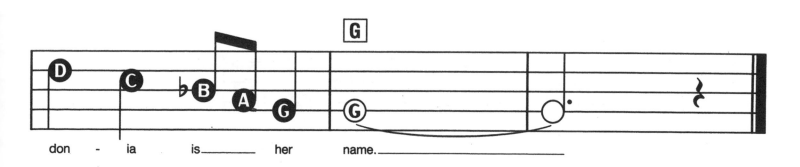

don - ia is____ her name.____

Early in the Mornin'

Registration 4
Rhythm: Blues

Words and Music by Leo Hickman,
Louis Jordan and Dallas Bartley

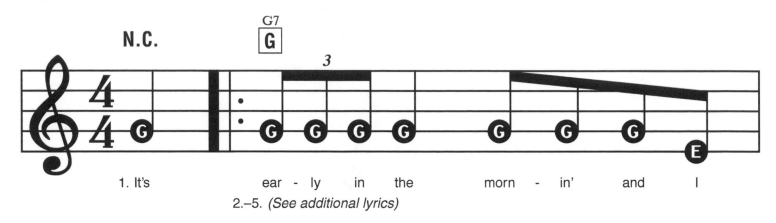

1. It's ear - ly in the morn - in' and I

2.–5. *(See additional lyrics)*

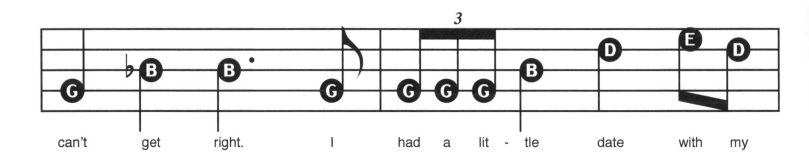

can't get right. I had a lit - tle date with my

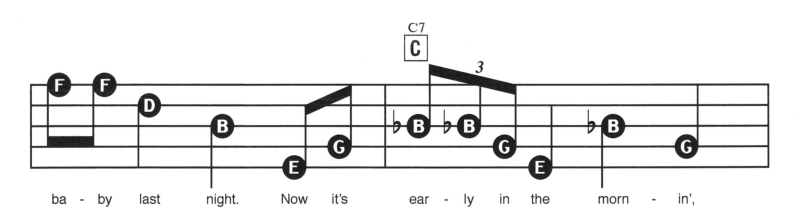

ba - by last night. Now it's ear - ly in the morn - in',

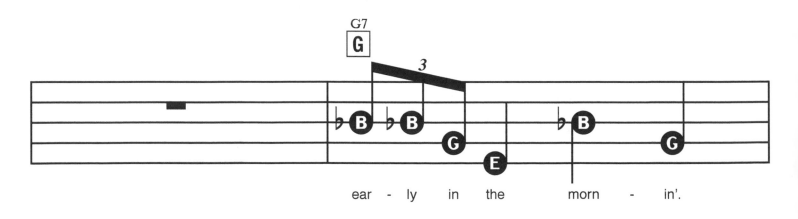

ear - ly in the morn - in'.

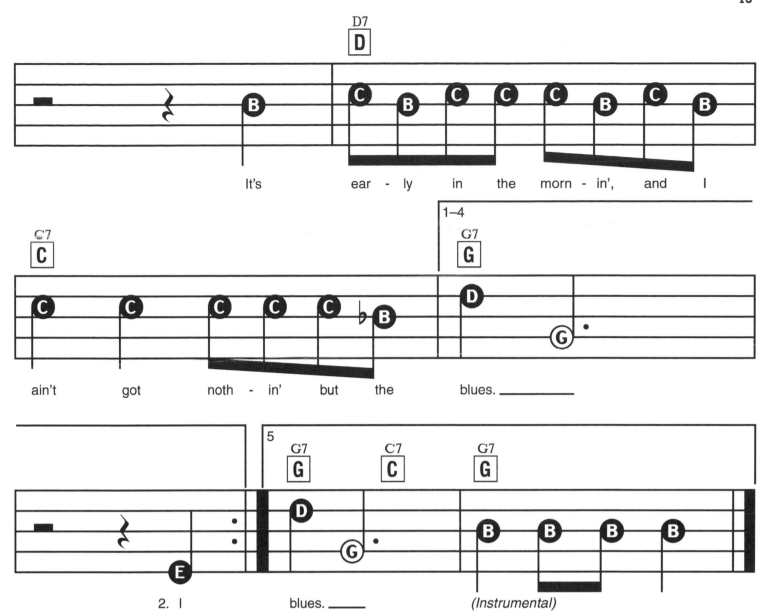

Additional Lyrics

2. I went to all the places where we used to go.
   Even went to her house, but she don't live there no more.
   It's early in the mornin', early in the mornin'.
   It's early in the mornin', and I ain't got nothin' but the blues.

3. I went to see her girlfriend, but she was out.
   Knocked on her mother's door, and she began to shout.
   (Spoken: "Get away from there, boy!")
   It's early in the mornin', early in the mornin'.
   It's early in the mornin', and I ain't got nothin' but the blues.

4. I went to Jenny Lou's to get something to eat.
   The waitress looked at me and said, "Pops, you sure look beat."
   It's early in the mornin', early in the mornin'.
   It's early in the mornin', and I ain't got nothin' but the blues.

5. I had a lot of money when I started out.
   Couldn't find my baby, now my money's run out.
   It's early in the mornin', early in the mornin'.
   It's early in the mornin', and I ain't got nothin' but the blues.

Every Day I Have the Blues

Registration 2
Rhythm: Fox Trot or Swing

Words and Music by
Peter Chatman

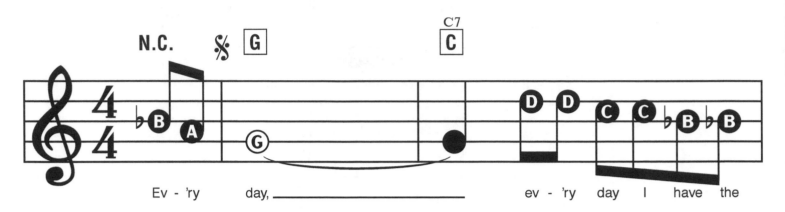

Ev - 'ry   day, _____   ev - 'ry day I   have the

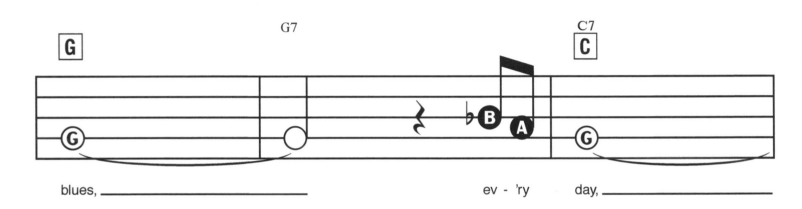

blues, _____   ev - 'ry   day, _____

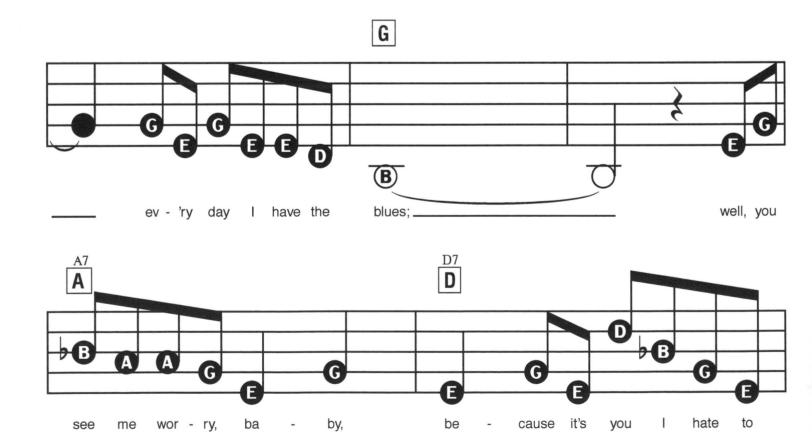

_____ ev - 'ry day I   have the   blues; _____   well, you

see me   wor - ry,   ba - by,   be - cause it's   you I   hate to

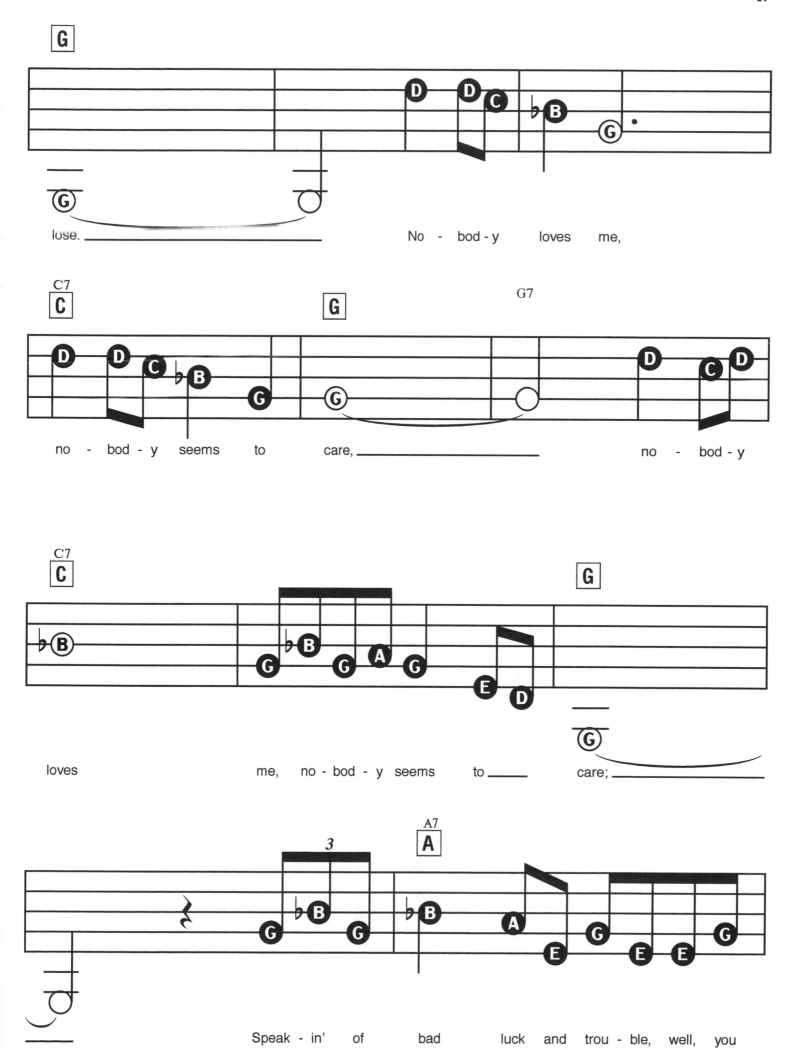

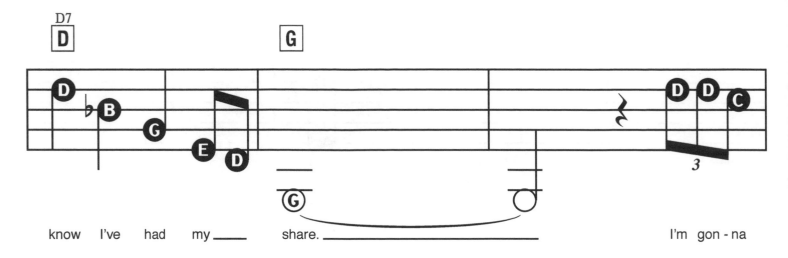

know I've had my ___ share. ___ I'm gon - na

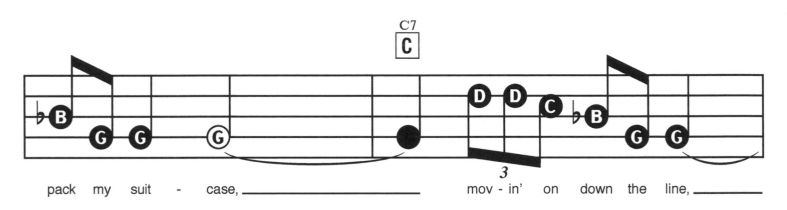

pack my suit - case, ___ mov - in' on down the line, ___

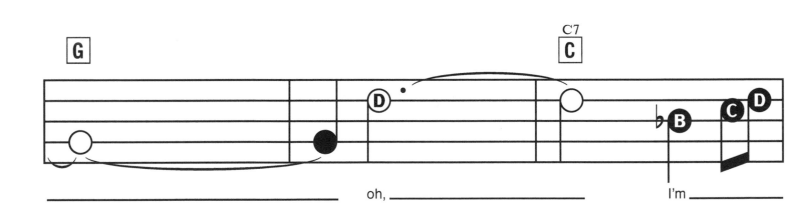

___ oh, ___ I'm ___

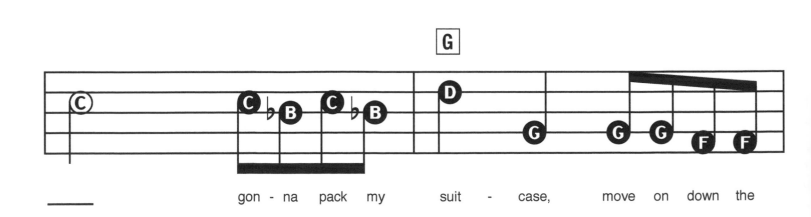

___ gon - na pack my suit - case, move on down the

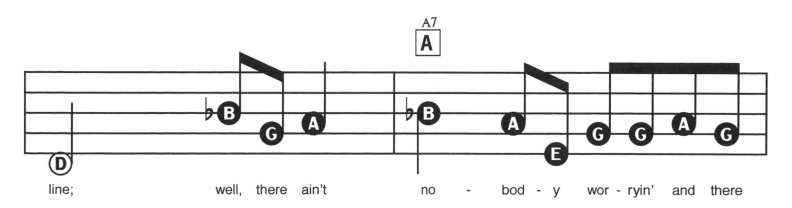

line; well, there ain't no - bod - y wor - ryin' and there

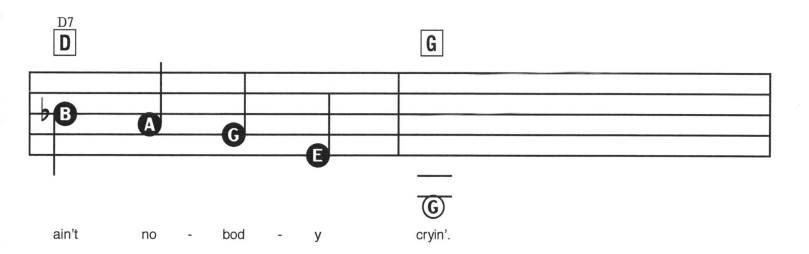

ain't no - bod - y cryin'.

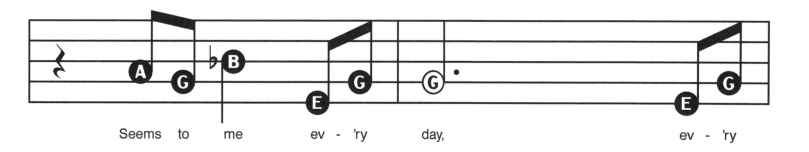

Seems to me ev - 'ry day, ev - 'ry

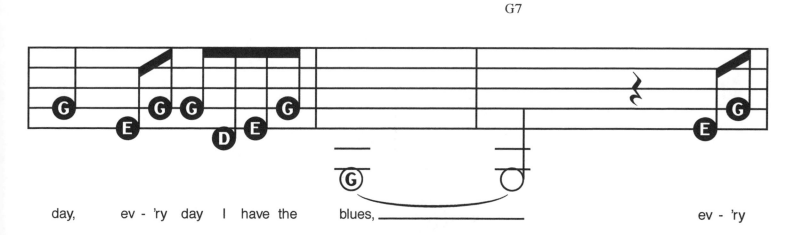

day, ev - 'ry day I have the blues, _____ ev - 'ry

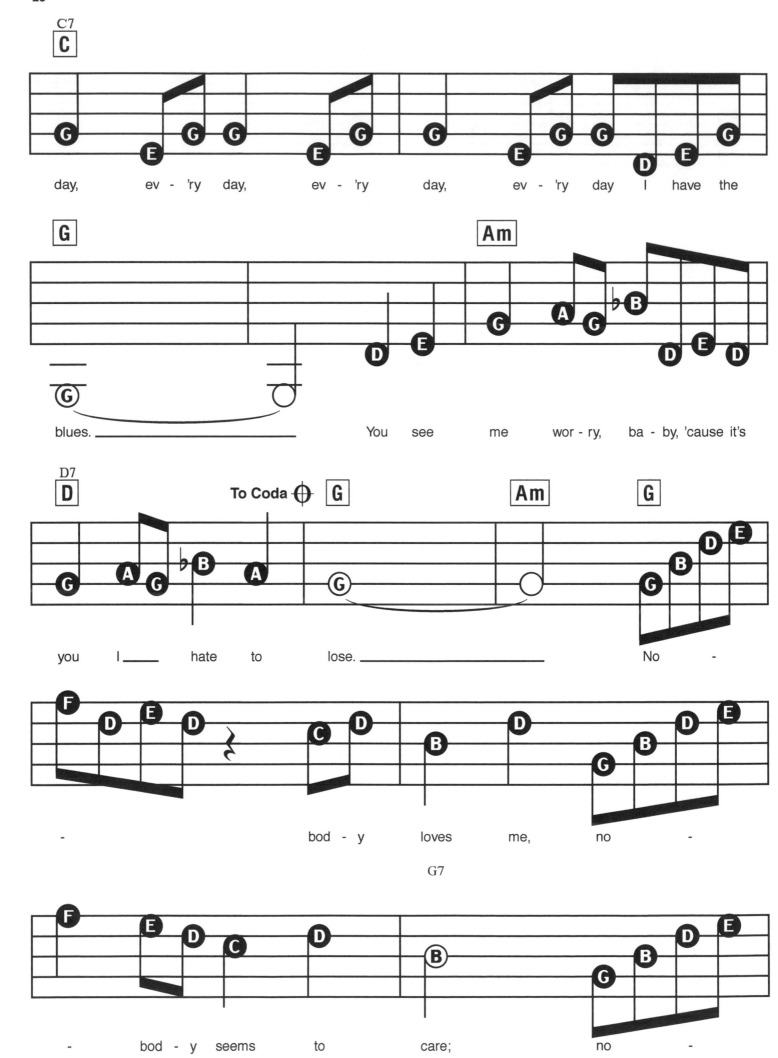

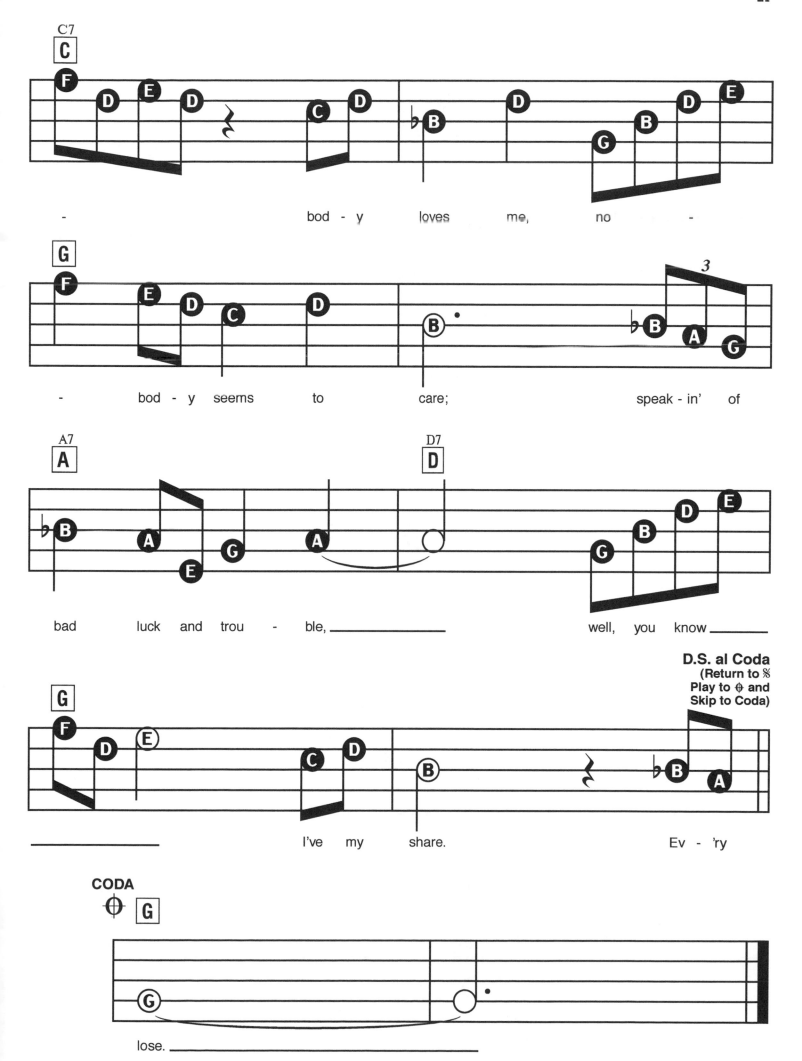

Fever

Registration 9
Rhythm: Fox Trot or Swing

Words and Music by John Davenport
and Eddie Cooley

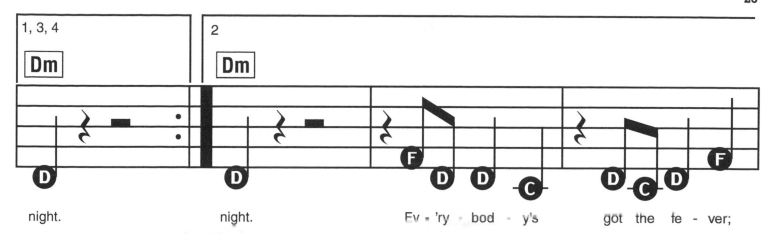

night.   night.   Ev - 'ry - bod - y's   got the fe - ver;

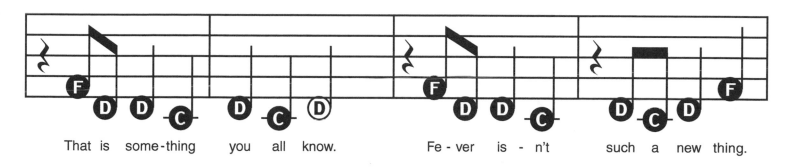

That is some - thing   you   all   know.   Fe - ver is - n't   such a new thing.

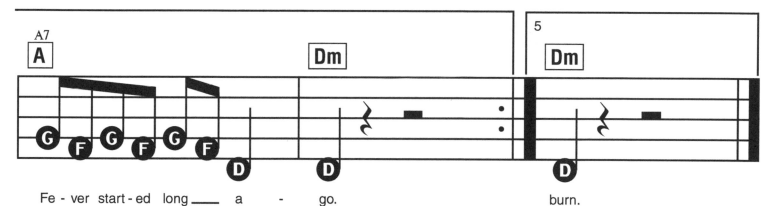

Fe - ver start - ed long___ a - go.   burn.

Additional Verses

Verse 3
Romeo loved Juliet,
Juliet, she felt the same.
When he put his arms around her, he said,
"Julie, baby, you're my flame."

Chorus
Thou givest fever when we kisseth,
Fever with thy flaming youth.
Fever — I'm afire,
Fever, yea I burn forsooth.

Verse 4
Captain Smith and Pocahontas
Had a very mad affair.
When her daddy tried to kill him, she said,
"Daddy-o, don't you dare."

Chorus
Give me fever with his kisses,
Fever when he holds me tight.
Fever — I'm his Missus,
Oh, Daddy, won't you treat him right.

Verse 5
Now you've listened to my story,
Here's the point that I have made.
Chicks were born to give you fever,
Be it fahrenheit or centigrade.

Chorus
They give you fever when you kiss them,
Fever if you live and learn.
Fever — till you sizzle,
What a lovely way to burn.

Gee Baby, Ain't I Good to You

Registration 7
Rhythm: Swing or Fox Trot

Words by Don Redman and Andy Razaf
Music by Don Redman

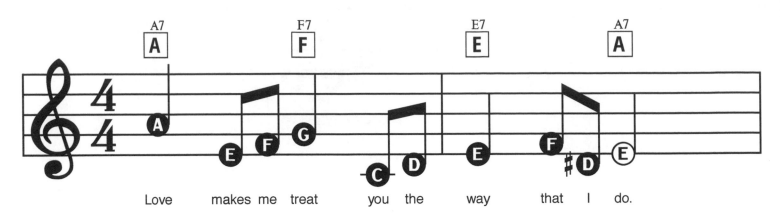

Love makes me treat you the way that I do.

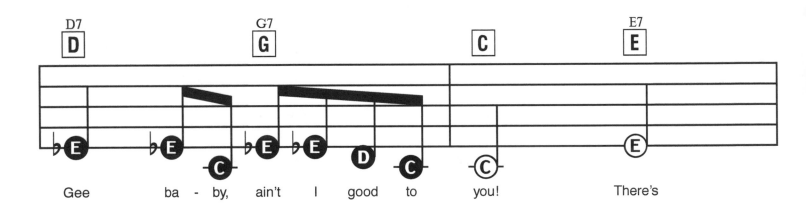

Gee ba - by, ain't I good to you! There's

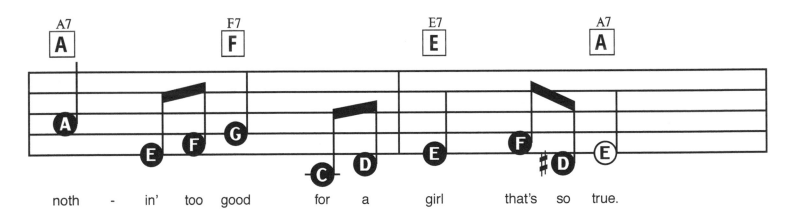

noth - in' too good for a girl that's so true.

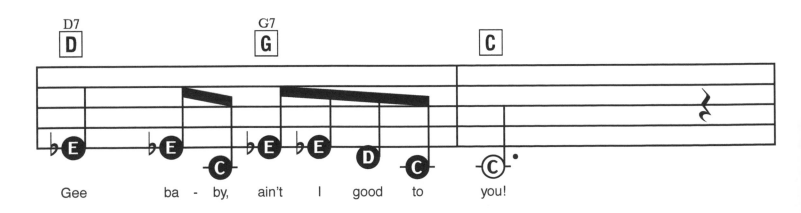

Gee ba - by, ain't I good to you!

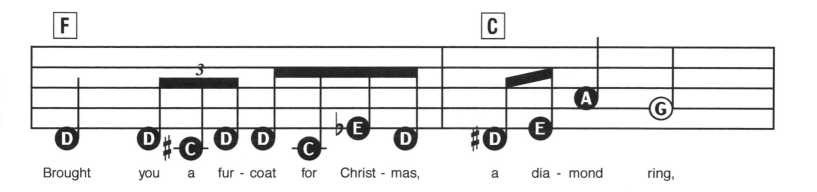

Brought you a fur-coat for Christ-mas, a dia-mond ring,

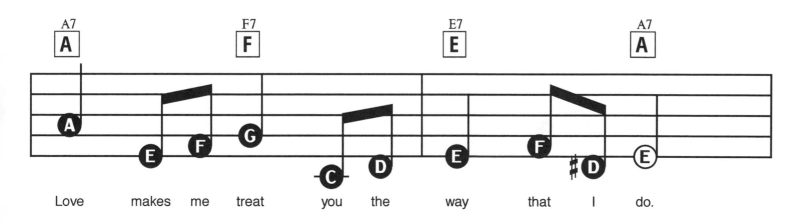

a Cad-il-lac car, an' ev-'ry-thing.

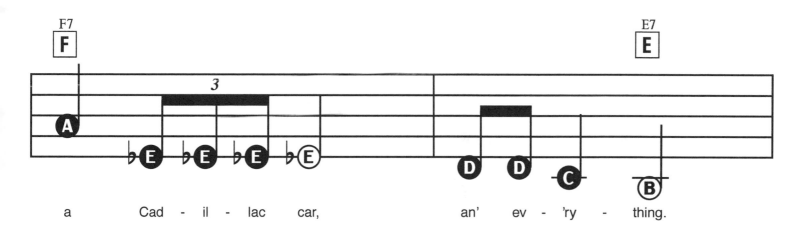

Love makes me treat you the way that I do.

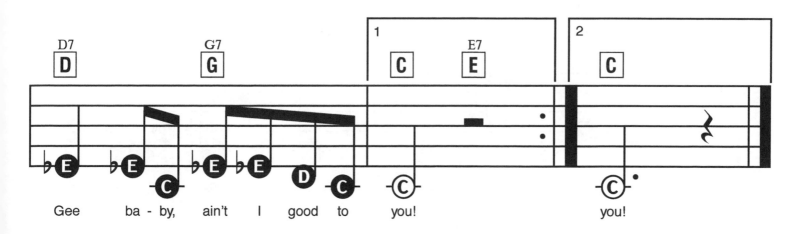

Gee ba-by, ain't I good to you!

you!

Good Morning Heartache

Registration 8
Rhythm: Fox Trot or Swing

Words and Music by Dan Fisher,
Irene Higginbotham and Ervin Drake

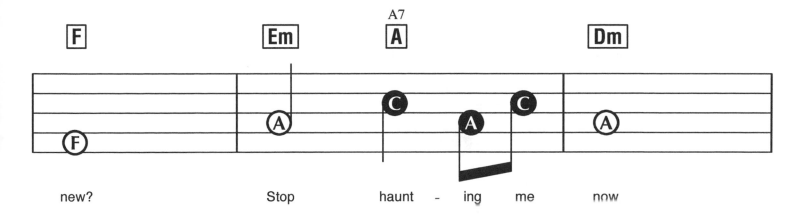

new?   Stop   haunt - ing   me   now

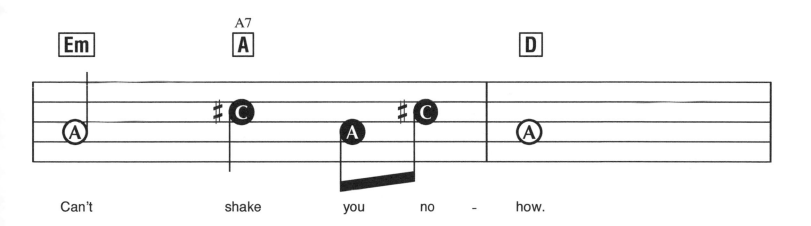

Can't   shake   you   no - how.

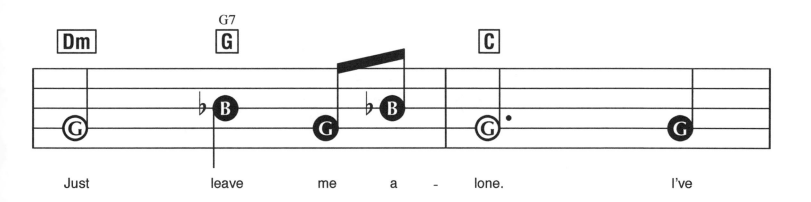

Just   leave   me   a - lone.   I've

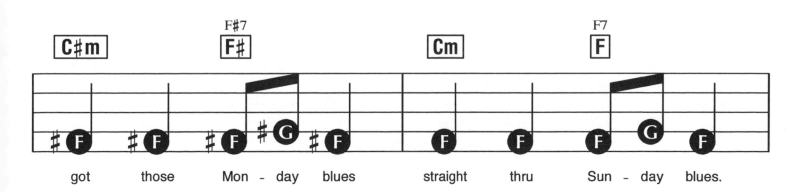

got   those   Mon - day   blues   straight   thru   Sun - day   blues.

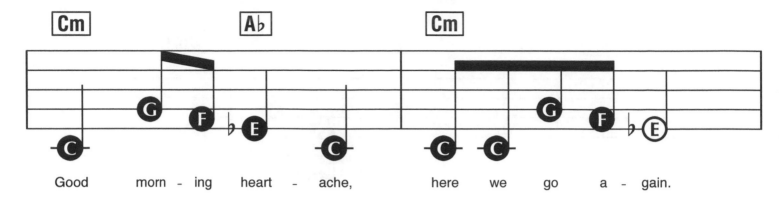

Good morn - ing heart - ache, here we go a - gain.

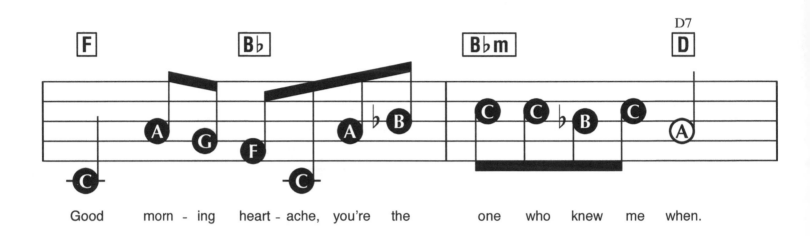

Good morn - ing heart - ache, you're the one who knew me when.

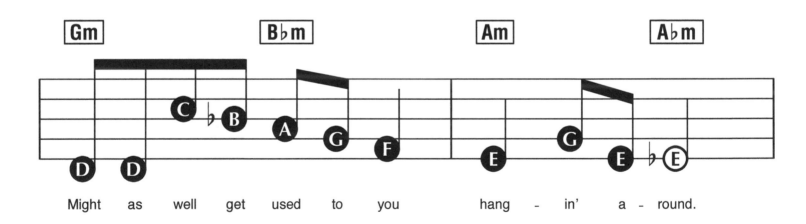

Might as well get used to you hang - in' a - round.

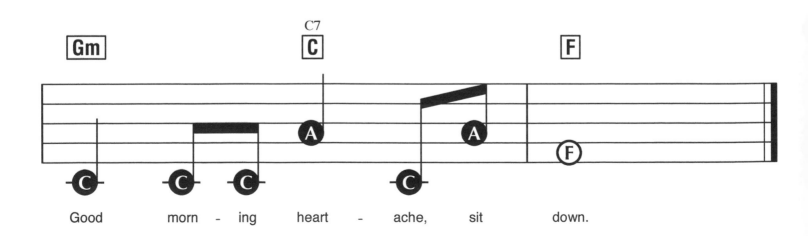

Good morn - ing heart - ache, sit down.

I'd Rather Go Blind

Registration 1
Rhythm: Waltz

Words and Music by Ellington Jordan
and Billy Foster

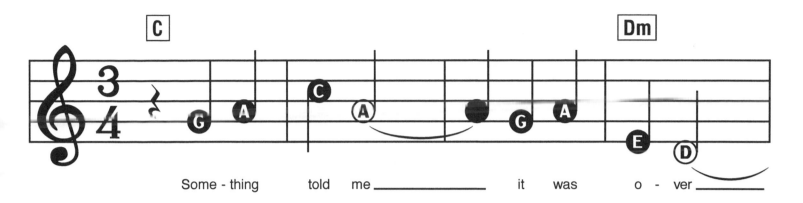

Some - thing   told   me _____   it   was   o - ver _____

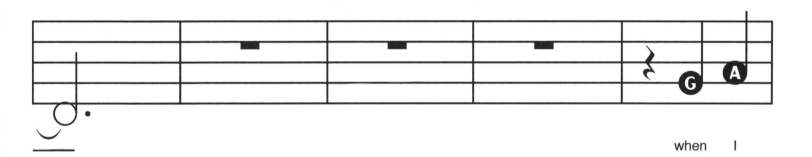

when   I

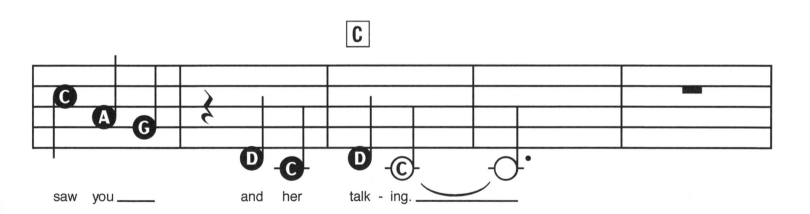

saw   you _____   and   her   talk - ing. _____

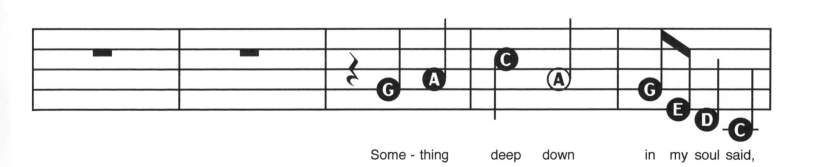

Some - thing   deep   down   in   my   soul   said,

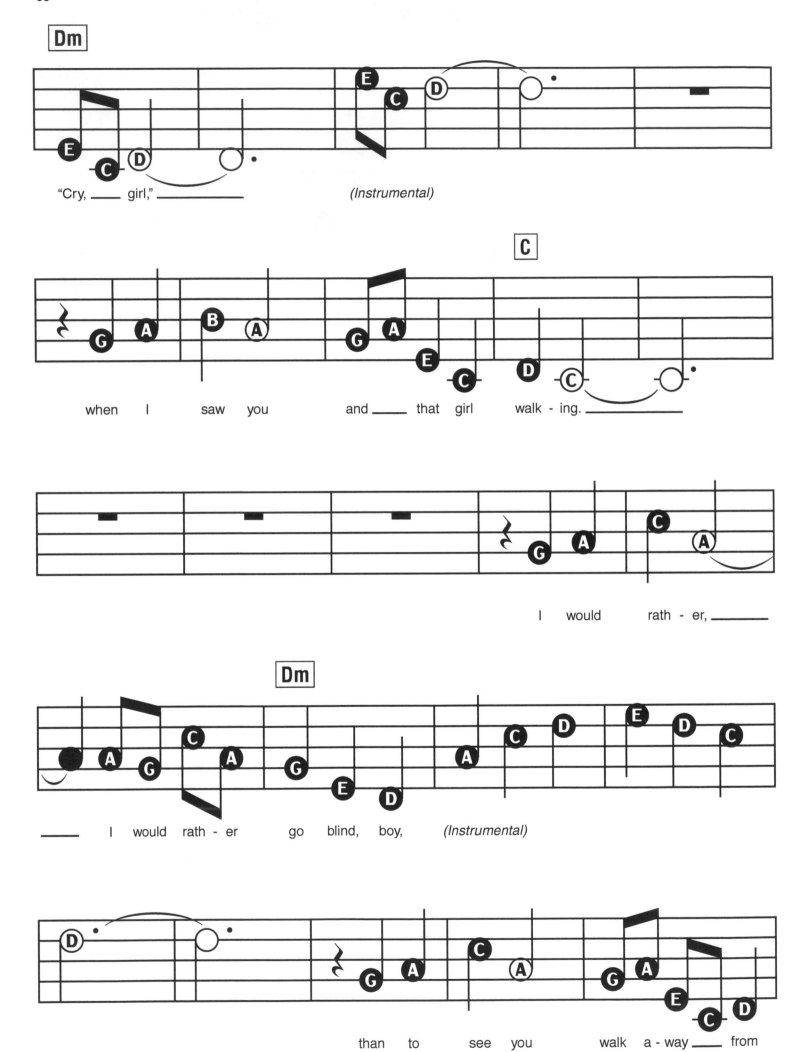

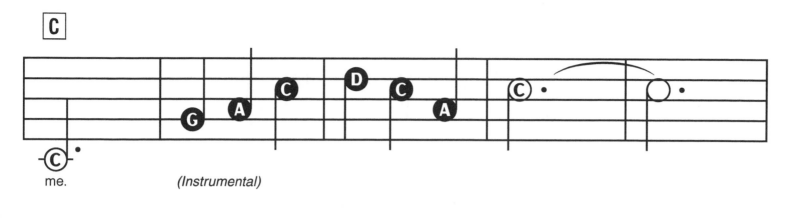

me.   (Instrumental)

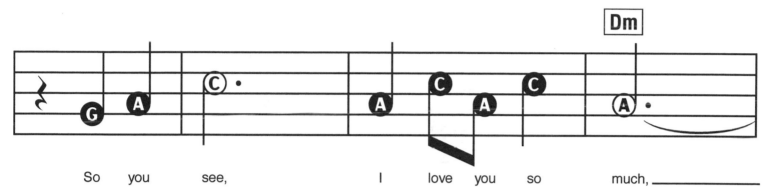

So you   see,   I   love you so   much, _____

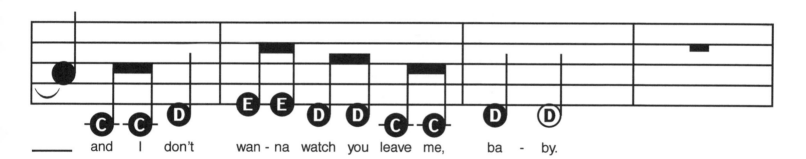

___ and I don't wan-na watch you leave me,   ba - by.

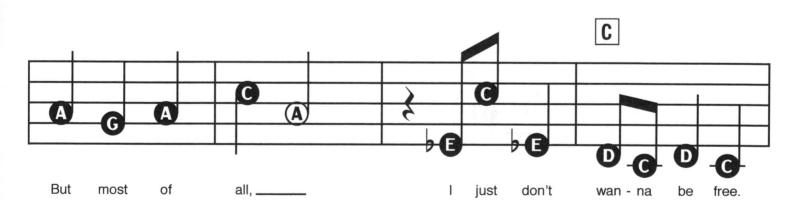

But most of   all, _____   I just don't wan-na be free.

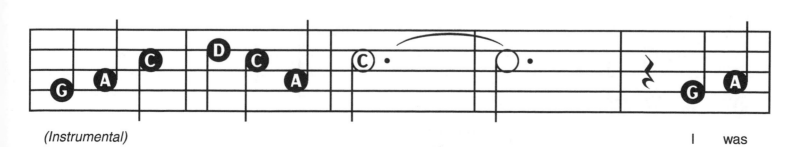

(Instrumental)   I was

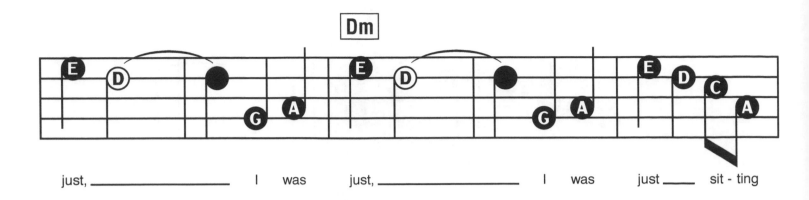

just, _____ I was just, _____ I was just ____ sit - ting

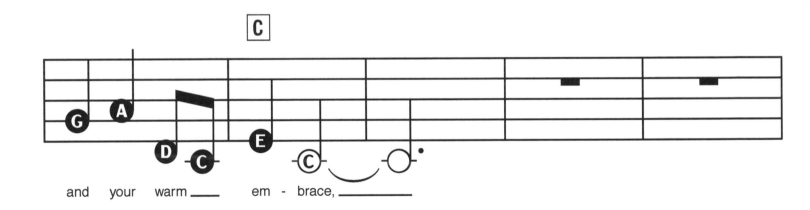

here think - ing _____ of your kiss _____

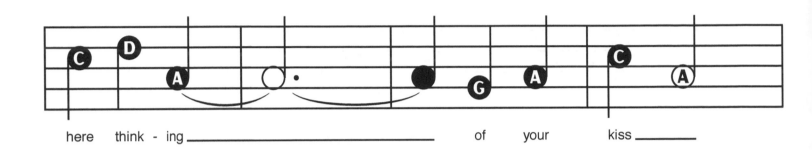

and your warm ____ em - brace, _____

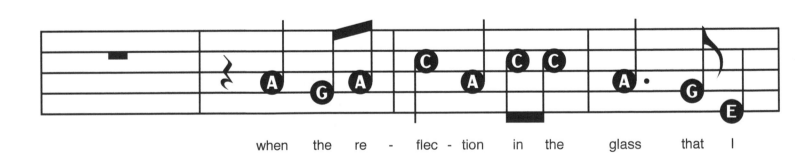

when the re - flec - tion in the glass that I

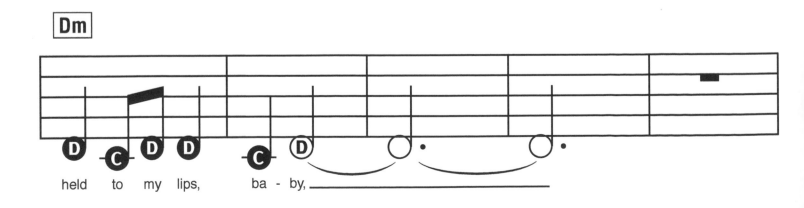

held to my lips, ba - by, _____

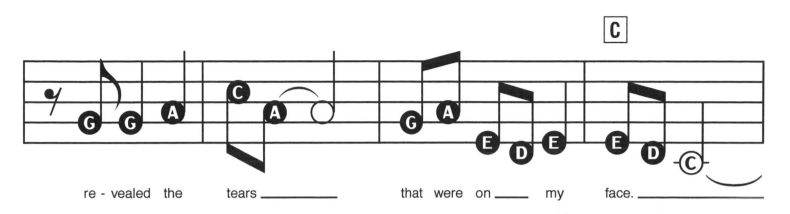

re - vealed the tears _____ that were on _____ my face. _____

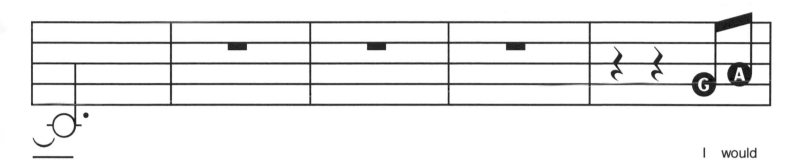

I would

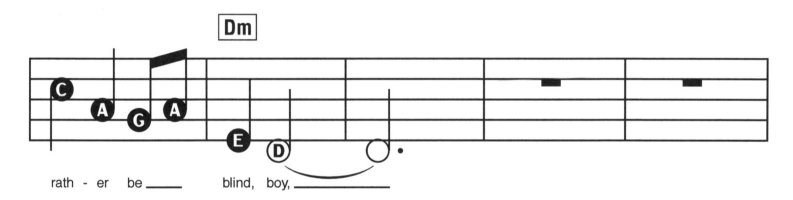

rath - er be _____ blind, boy, _____

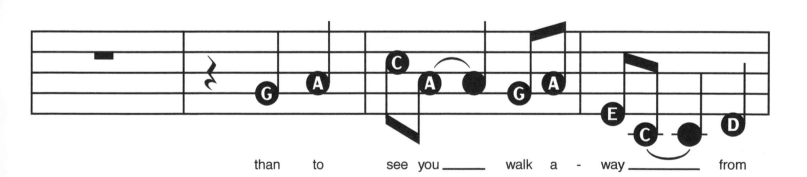

than to see you _____ walk a - way _____ from

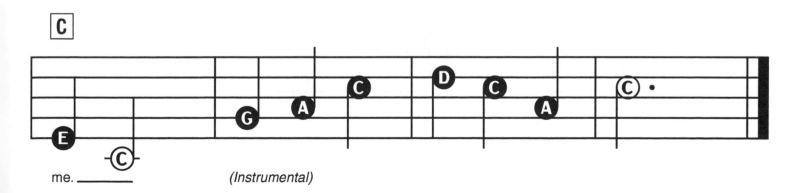

me. _____ *(Instrumental)*

Hi-Heel Sneakers

Registration 4
Rhythm: Rock or Blues

Words and Music by
Robert Higgenbotham

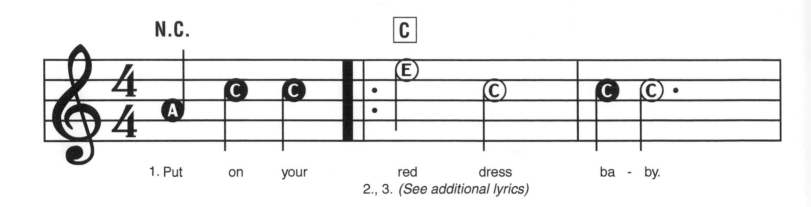

1. Put on your red dress ba - by.
2., 3. *(See additional lyrics)*

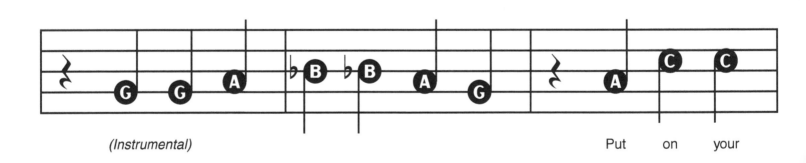

Lord, we're go - in' out to - night.

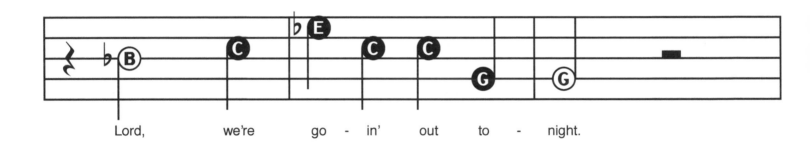

(Instrumental)   Put on your

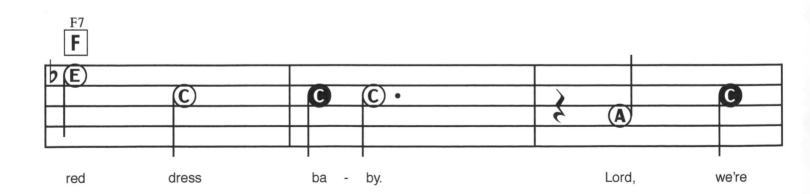

red dress ba - by.   Lord, we're

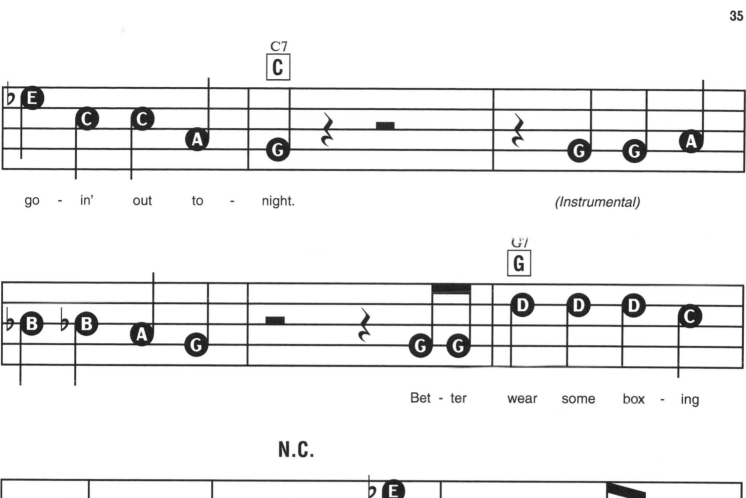

go - in' out to - night.   (Instrumental)

Bet - ter   wear   some   box - ing

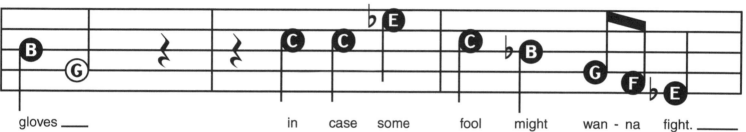

gloves ____   in   case   some   fool   might   wan - na   fight. ____

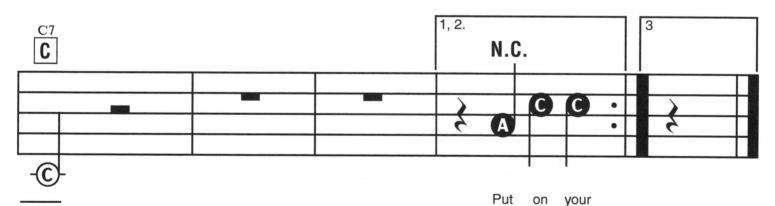

Put   on   your

Additional Lyrics

2. Put on your high heel sneakers, wear your wig hat on your head.
   Put on your high heel sneakers, wear your wig hat on your head.
   And I'm pretty sure, now, baby,
   Lord, you know, you know you're gonna knock 'em dead.

3. Put on your high heel sneakers, wear your wig hat on your head.
   Put on your high heel sneakers, wear your wig hat on your head.
   Know you oughtta realize
   I'm pretty sure you're gonna knock 'em dead.

I Ain't Got Nobody
(And Nobody Cares for Me)

Registration 8
Rhythm: Swing or Shuffle

Words by Roger Graham
Music by Spencer Williams and Dave Peyton

N.C.

G7 — G

A7 — A

Now I _____ ain't got no - bod -

G

A7 — A

D7 — D

y, and _____ no - bod - y cares for

G

D7 — D

G7 — G

me. And _____ I'm sad and

A7 — A

lone - ly, won't some - bod - y

D

come and take a chance with me?

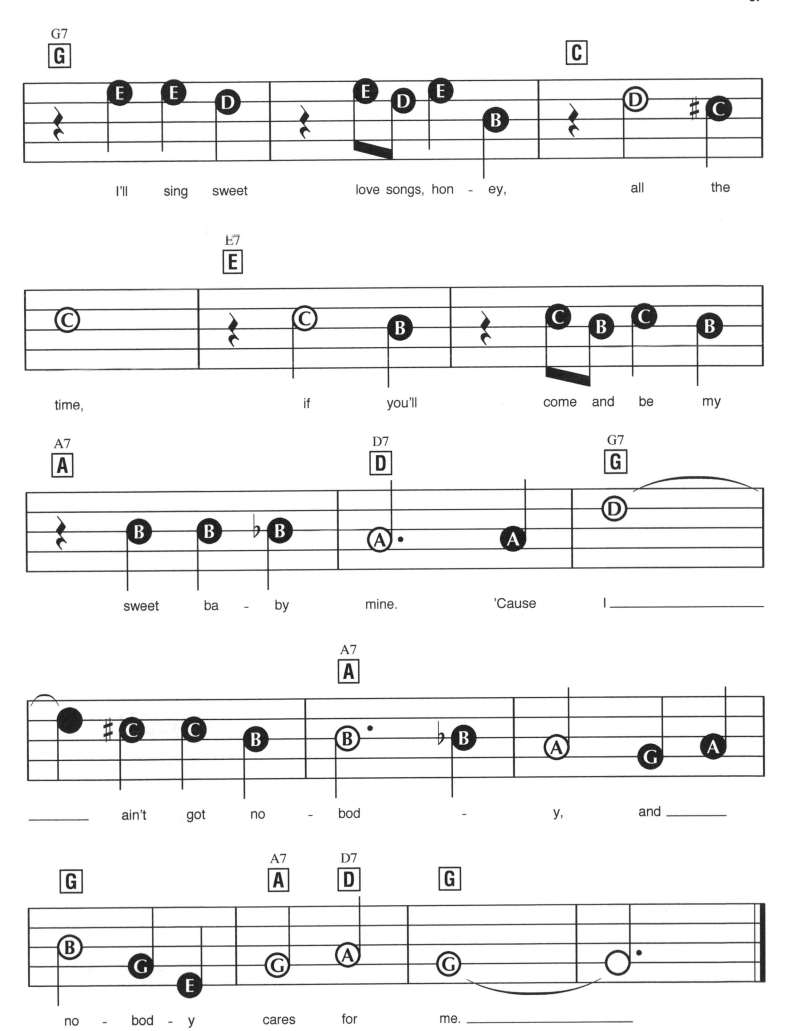

I Almost Lost My Mind

Registration 4
Rhythm: Slow Rock or Rock

Words and Music by
Ivory Joe Hunter

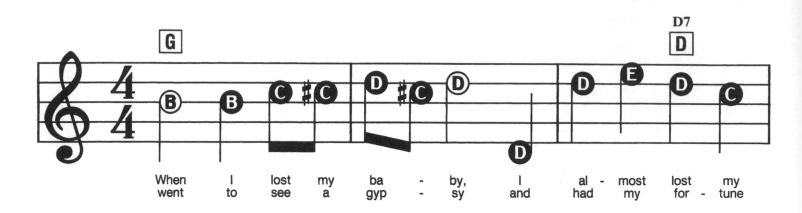

When I lost my ba - by, I al - most lost my
went to see a gyp - sy and had my for - tune

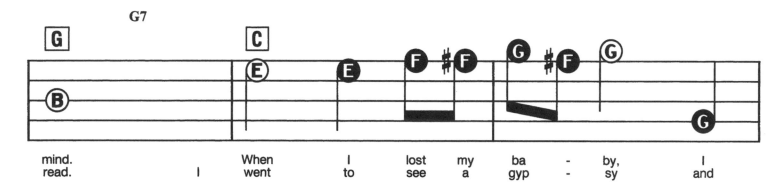

mind. When I lost my ba - by, I
read. I went to see a gyp - sy and

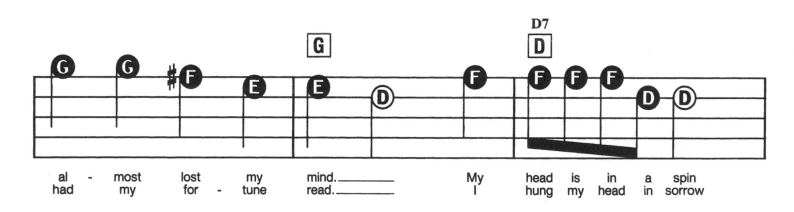

al - most lost my mind._____ My head is in a spin
had my for - tune read._____ I hung my head in sorrow

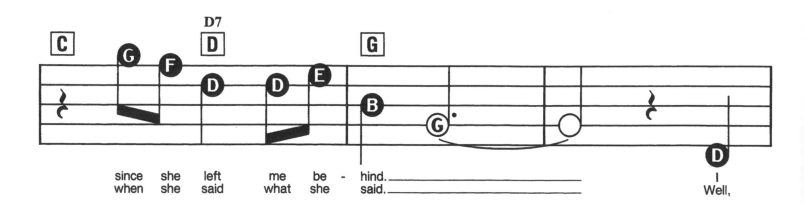

since she left me be - hind._____
when she said what she said._____ Well,

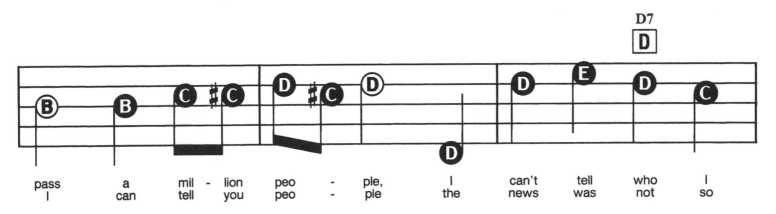

pass   a   mil - lion   peo - ple,   I   can't   tell   who   I
I   can   tell   you   peo - ple   the   news   was   not   so

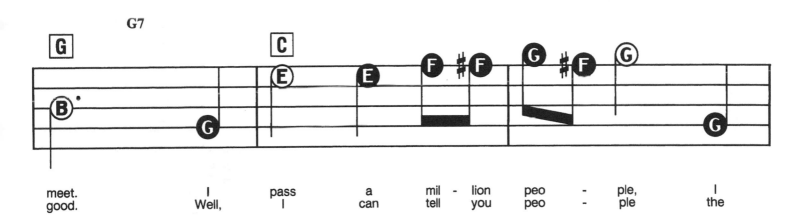

meet.   I   pass   a   mil - lion   peo - ple,   I
good.   Well, I   can   tell   you   peo - ple   the

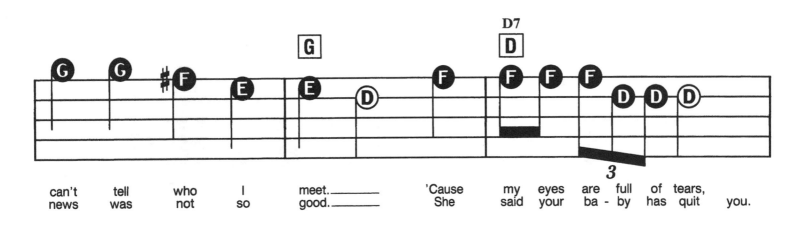

can't   tell   who   I   meet._____   'Cause   my   eyes   are full   of tears,
news   tell   was   not   so   good._____   She   said your ba - by   has quit   you.

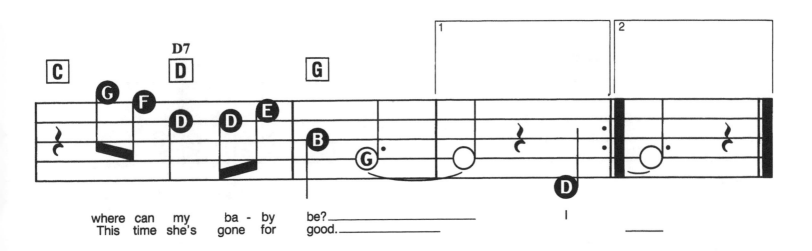

where can my   ba - by   be?_____
This time she's gone for good._____

I Got It Bad and That Ain't Good

Registration 6
Rhythm: Ballad

Words by Paul Francis Webster
Music by Duke Ellington

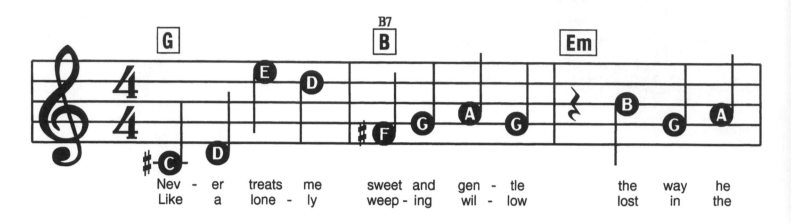

Nev - er treats me sweet and gen - tle the way he
Like a lone - ly weep - ing wil - low lost in the

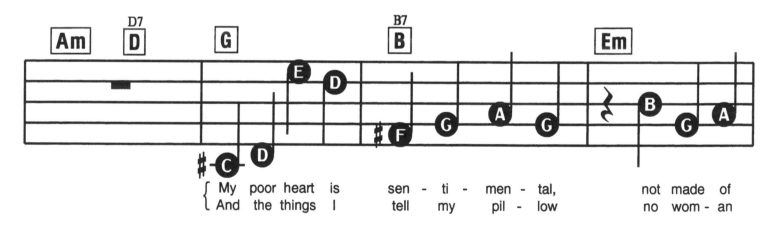

should;
wood,
I got it bad and that ain't good!

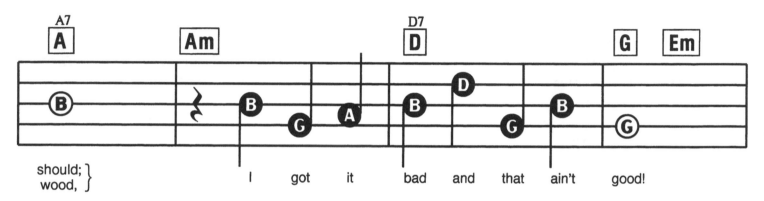

My poor heart is sen - ti - men - tal, not made of
And the things I tell my pil - low no wom - an

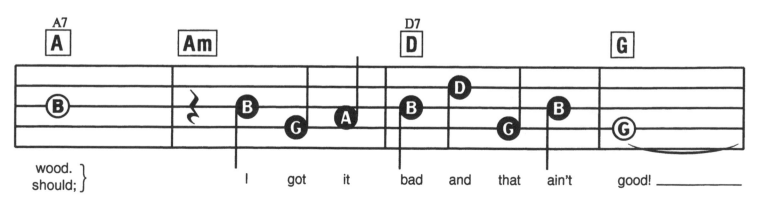

wood.
should;
I got it bad and that ain't good! _____

But when the week-end's o-ver and Mon-day rolls a-
Though folks with good in-ten-tions tell me to save my

round, I end up like I start out just cry-in' my
tears, I'm glad I'm mad a-bout him, I can't live with-

heart out.
out him. He don't love me, like I love him;
Lord a-bove me, make him love me

no-bod-y could.
the way he should.   I got it bad and that ain't

1
good! _____

2
good! _____

I'm Your Hoochie Coochie Man

Registration 4
Rhythm: Blues or Rock

Written by Willie Dixon

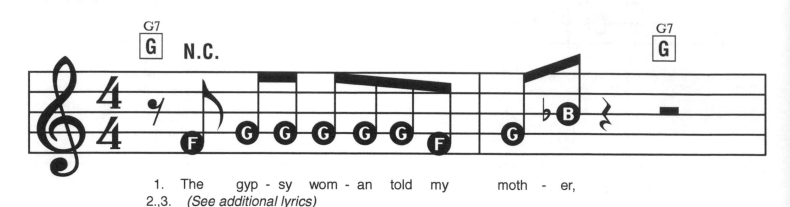

1. The gyp - sy wom - an told my moth - er,
2.,3. *(See additional lyrics)*

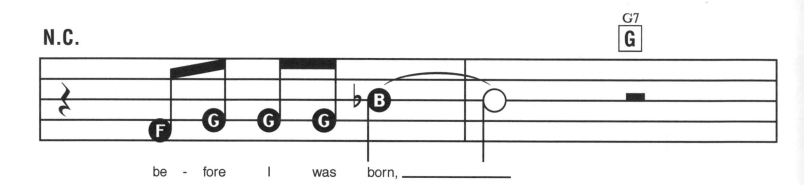

be - fore I was born, _____

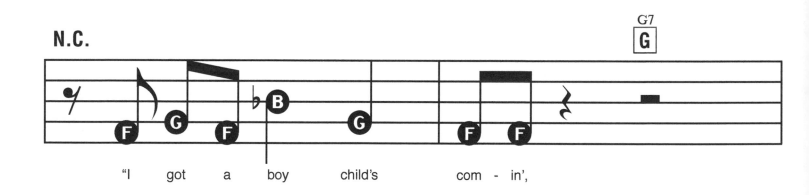

"I got a boy child's com - in',

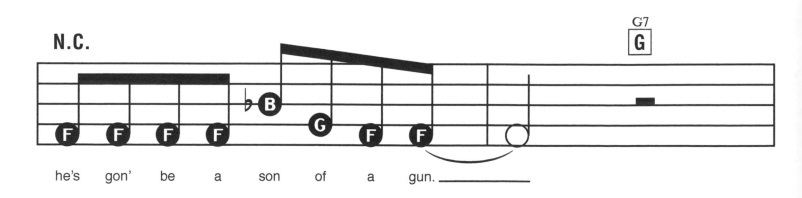

he's gon' be a son of a gun. _____

43

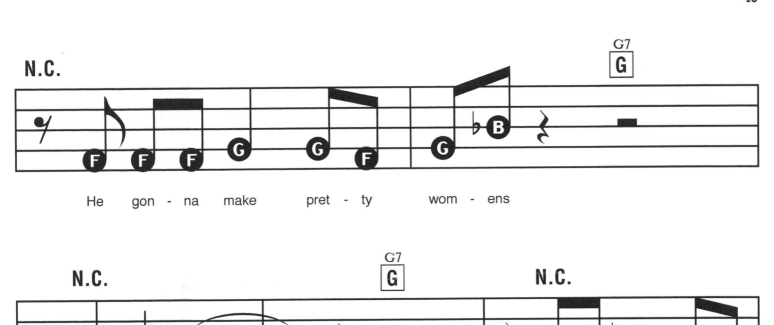

He gon - na make pret - ty wom - ens

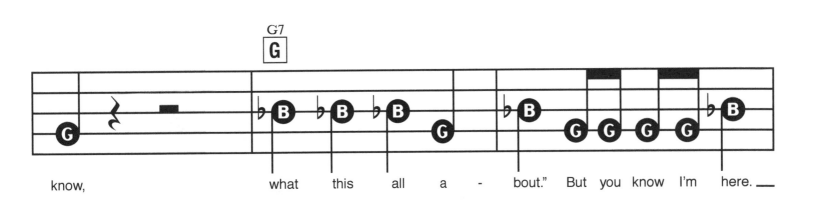

jump and shout. _____ Then the world wan - na

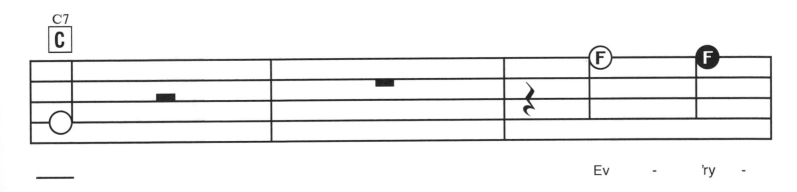

know, what this all a - bout." But you know I'm here. __

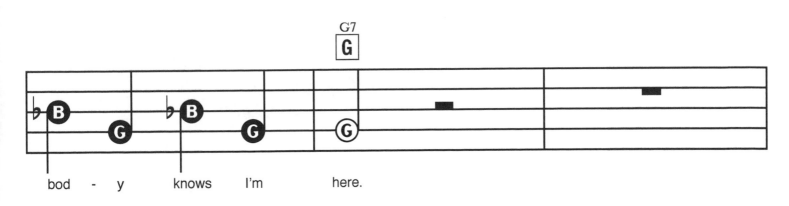

___ Ev - 'ry -

bod - y knows I'm here.

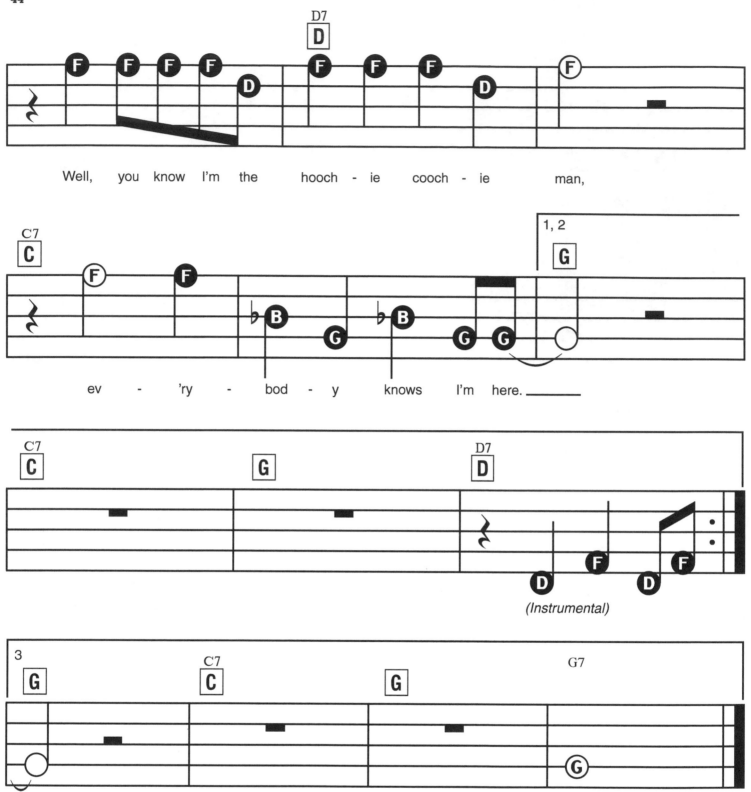

(Instrumental)

Additional Lyrics

2. I got a black cat bone, I got a mojo too,
   I got the John the Conquer'r root, I'm gonna mess with you.
   I'm gonna make you girls lead me by my hand,
   Then the world'll know the hoochie coochie man.

3. On the seventh hour, on the seventh day,
   On the seventh month, the seventh doctor say,
   "He was born for good luck, and that you'll see."
   I got seven hundred dollars; don't you mess with me.

St. Louis Blues
from BIRTH OF THE BLUES

Registration 7
Rhythm: Swing

Words and Music by
W.C. Handy

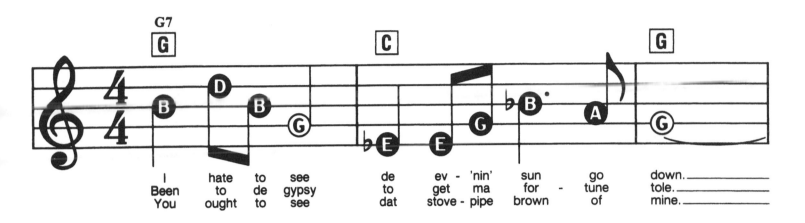

I hate to see de ev - 'nin' sun go down. _____
Been to de gypsy to get ma for - tune tole. _____
You ought to see gypsy dat stove - pipe brown of mine. _____

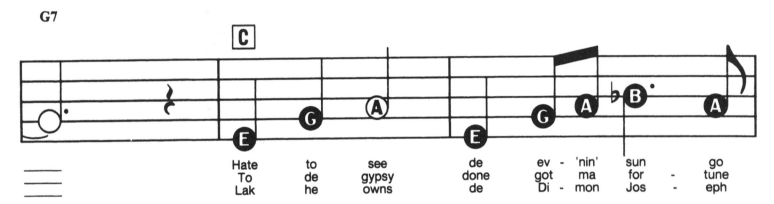

Hate to see de ev - 'nin' sun go
To de gypsy done got ma for - tune
Lak he owns de Di - mon Jos - eph

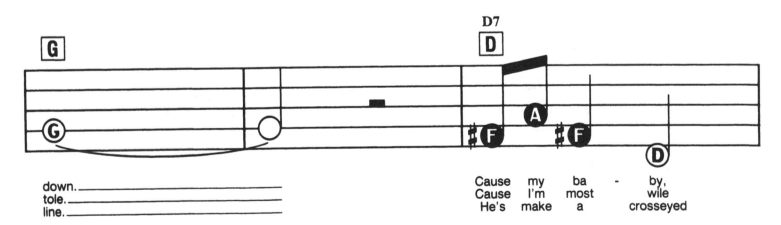

down. _____
tole. _____
line. _____

Cause my ba - by,
Cause I'm most wile
He's make a crosseyed

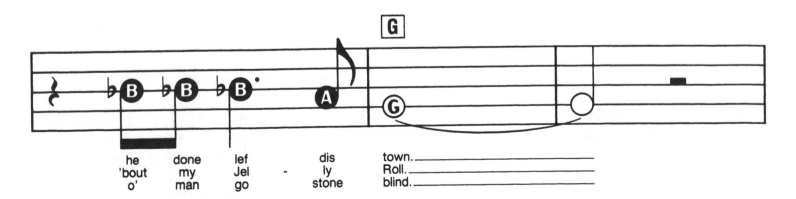

he done lef dis town. _____
'bout my Jel - ly Roll. _____
o' man go stone blind. _____

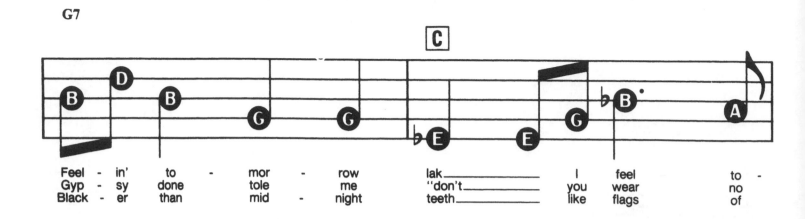

Feel - in' to - mor - row lak_____ I feel to -
Gyp - sy done tole me "don't_____ you wear no
Black - er than mid - night teeth_____ like flags of

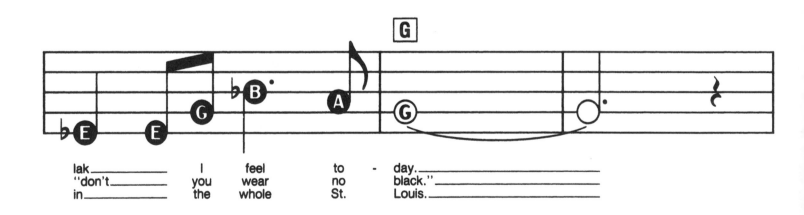

day._____ Feel to - mor - row
black."_____ Yes she done tole me
truce._____ Black - est man

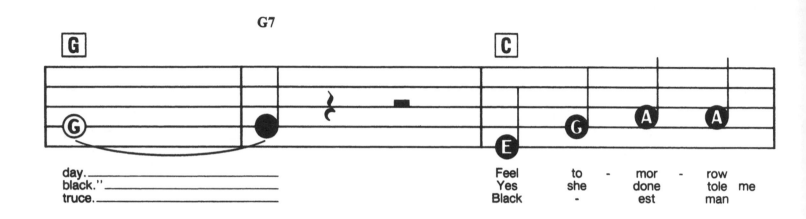

lak_____ I feel to - day._____
"don't_____ you wear no black."_____
in_____ the whole St. Louis._____

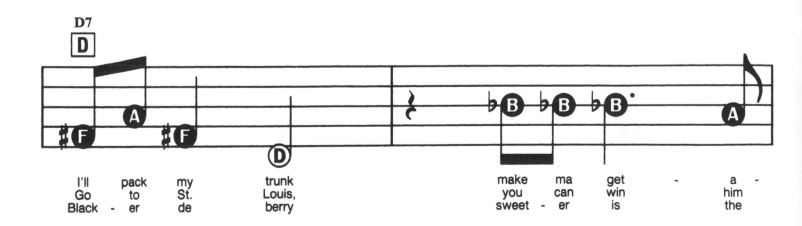

I'll pack my trunk make ma can get win - a -
Go to St. Louis, you sweet - er is him
Black - er de berry

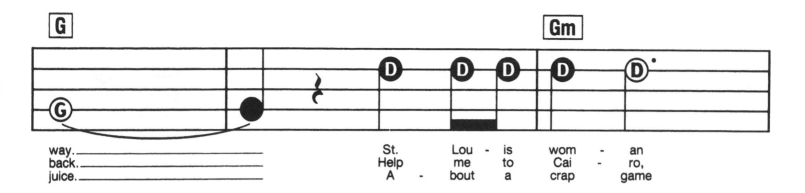

G ... **Gm**

way._____
back._____
juice._____

St. Lou - is wom - an
Help me to Cai - ro,
A - bout a crap game

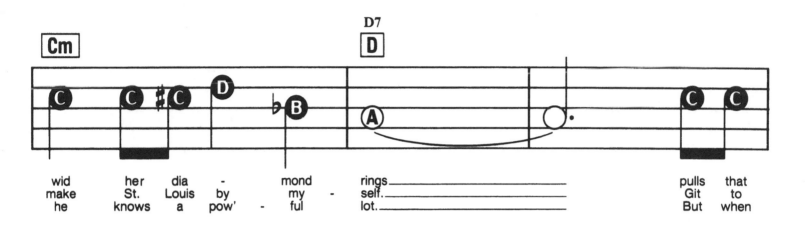

Cm ... **D7** **D**

wid her dia - mond rings_____ pulls that
make St. Louis by my - self._____ Git to
he knows a pow' - ful lot._____ But when

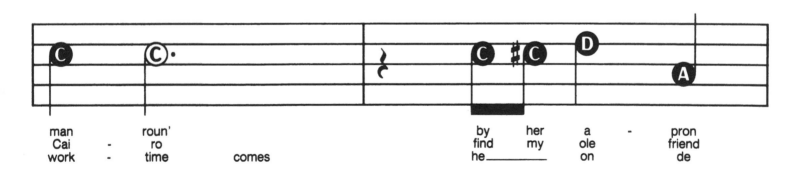

man roun' by her a - pron
Cai - ro find my ole friend
work - time comes he_____ on de

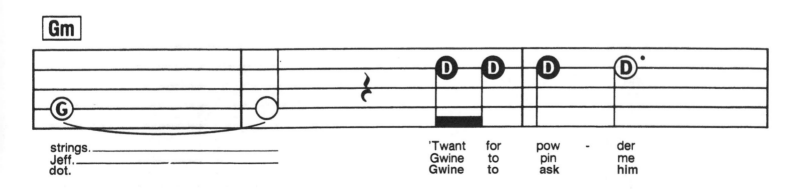

Gm

strings._____
Jeff._____
dot._____

'Twant for pow - der
Gwine to pin me
Gwine to ask him

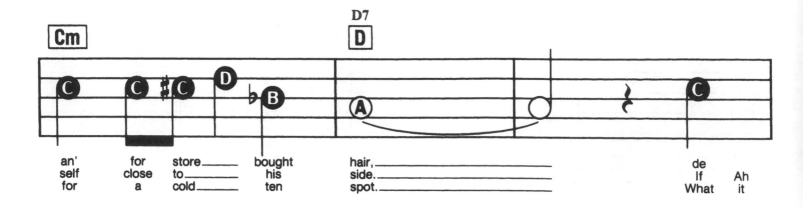

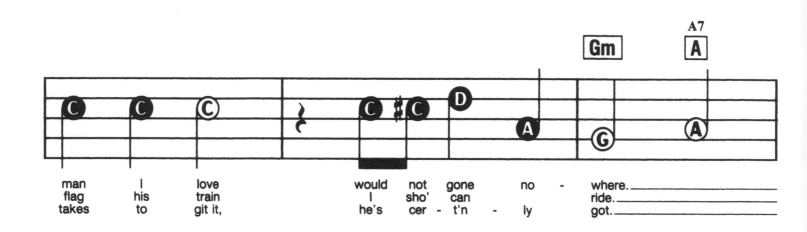

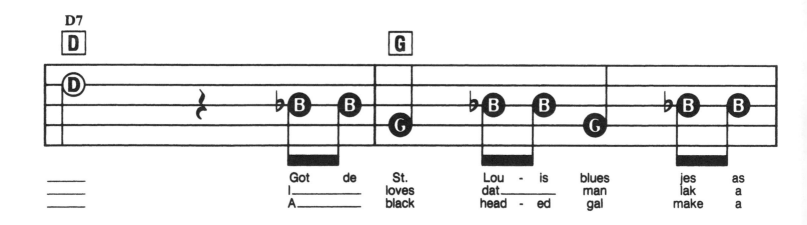

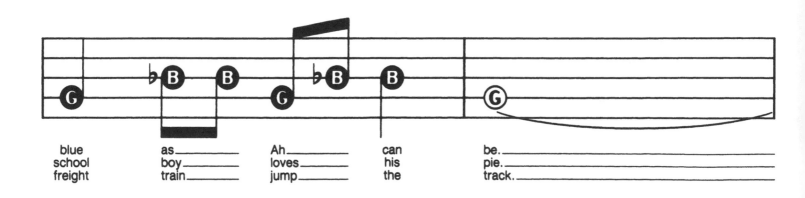

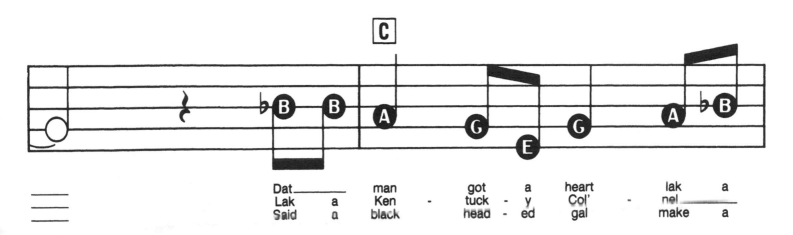

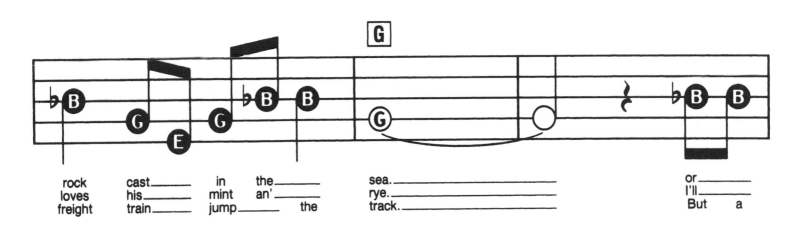

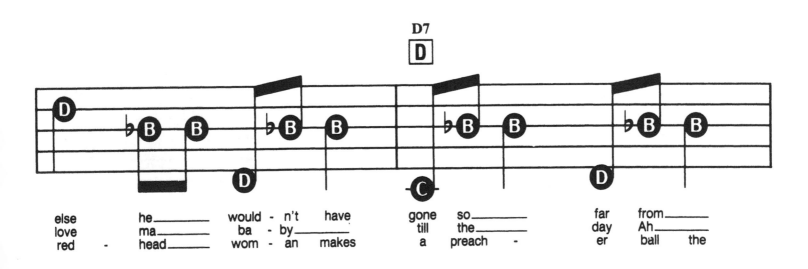

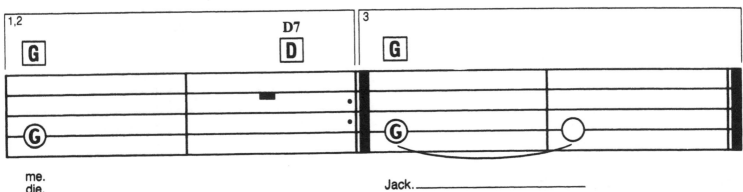

It Hurts Me Too

Registration 4
Rhythm: Shuffle or Blues

Words and Music by
Mel London

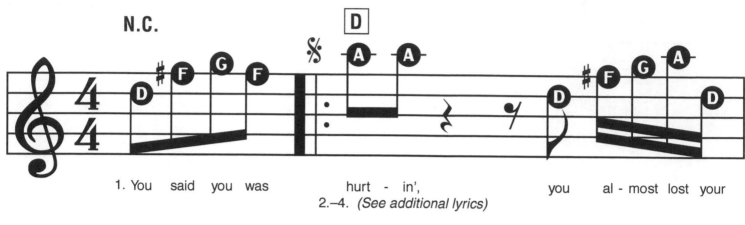

1. You said you was hurt - in', you al - most lost your
2.–4. *(See additional lyrics)*

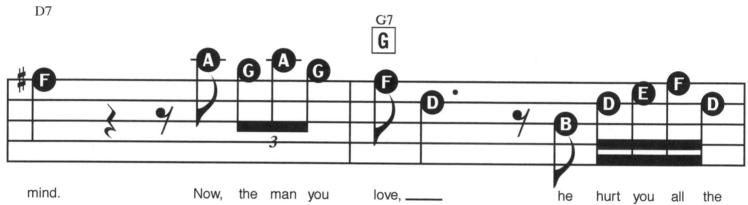

mind. Now, the man you love, _____ he hurt you all the

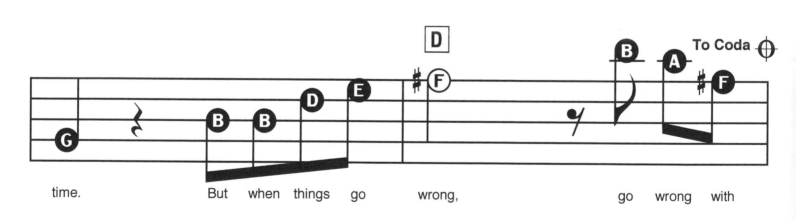

time. But when things go wrong, go wrong with

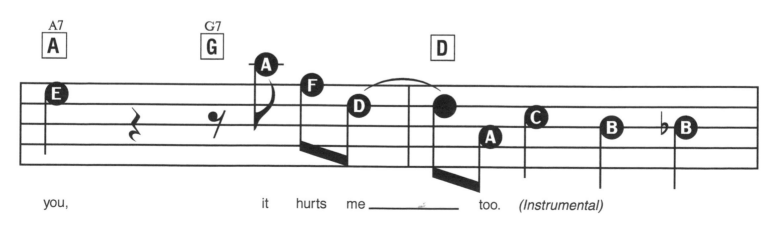

you, it hurts me _____ too. *(Instrumental)*

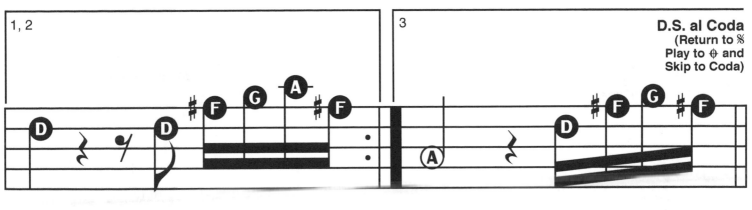

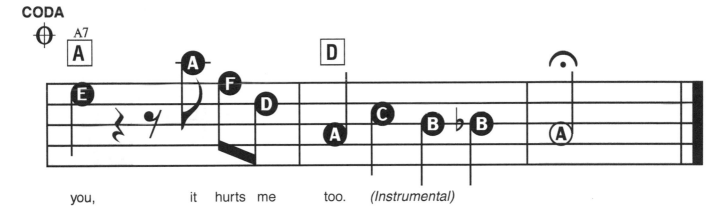

Additional Lyrics

2. You'll love him more when you should love him less.
   Why pick up behind him, and take his mess?
   But when things go wrong, go wrong with you,
   It hurts me too.

3. He love another woman. Yes, I love you.
   But you love him, and stick to him like glue.
   But when things go wrong, go wrong with you,
   It hurts me too.

4. Now, he better leave you or you better put him down.
   No, I won't stand to see you pushed around.
   But when things go wrong, go wrong with you,
   It hurts me too.

Kansas City

Registration 4
Rhythm: Shuffle or Swing

Words and Music by Jerry Leiber
and Mike Stoller

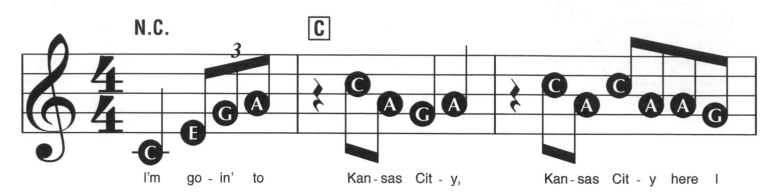

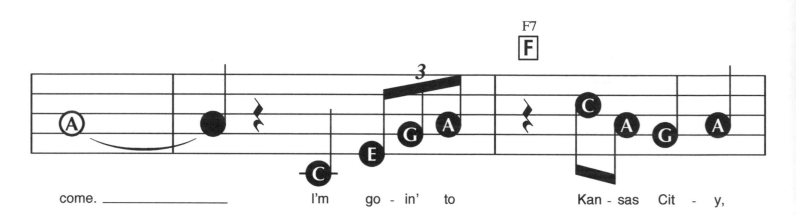

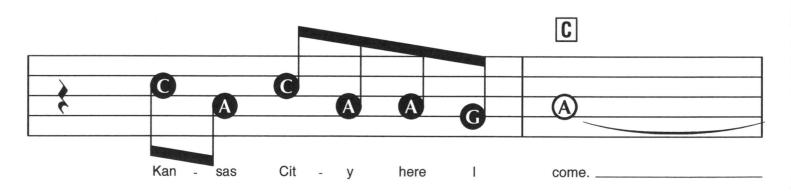

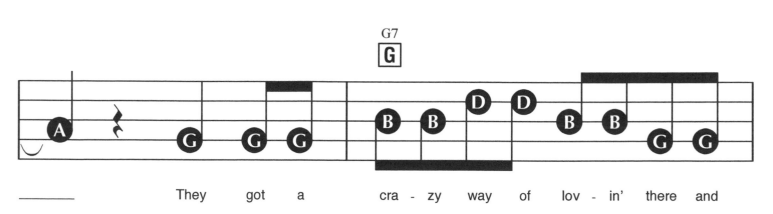

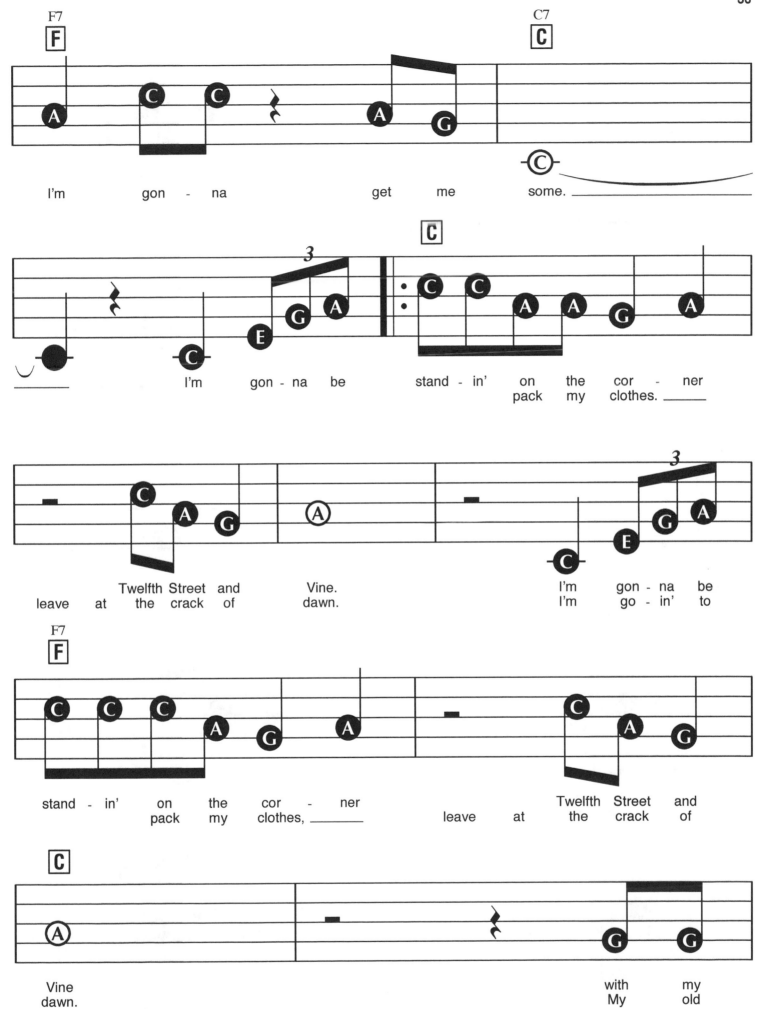

Let the Good Times Roll

Registration 8
Rhythm: Blues or Swing

Words and Music by Sam Theard
and Fleecie Moore

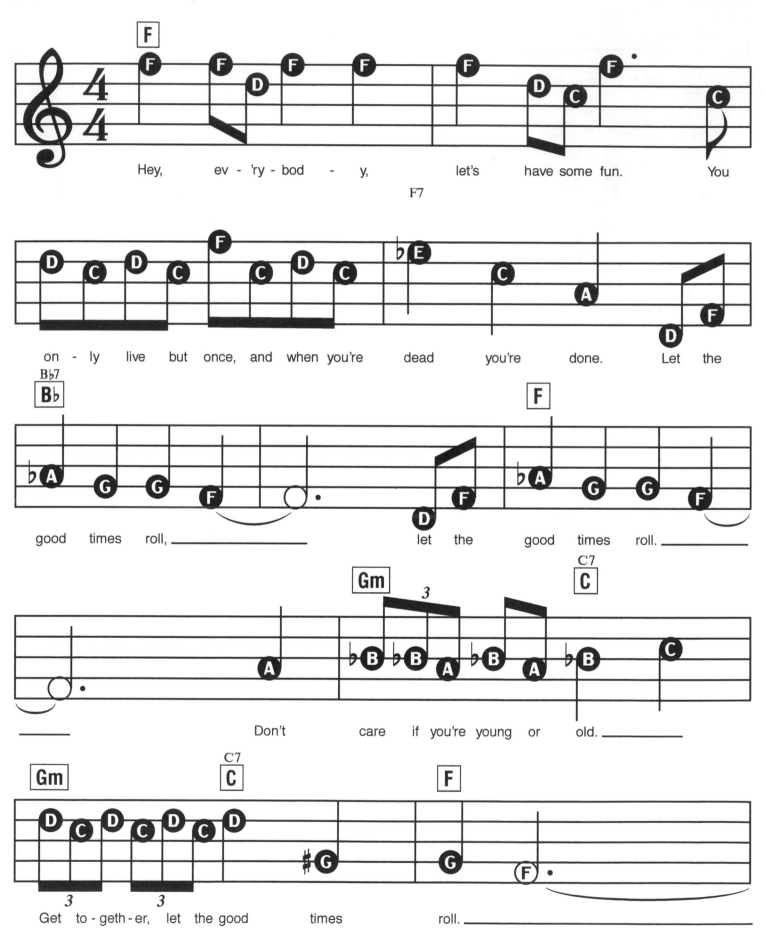

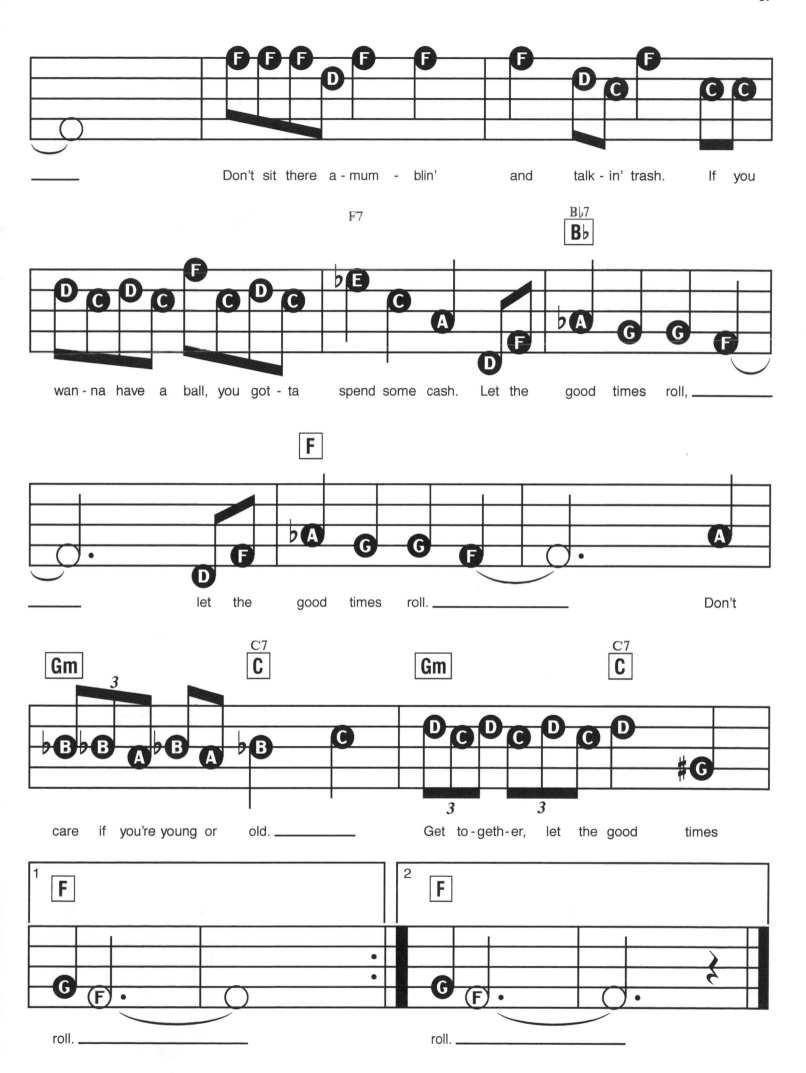

My Babe

Registration 4
Rhythm: Shuffle or Blues

Written by Willie Dixon

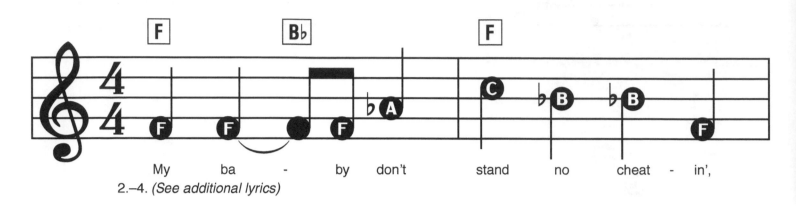

My ba - by don't stand no cheat - in',
2.–4. *(See additional lyrics)*

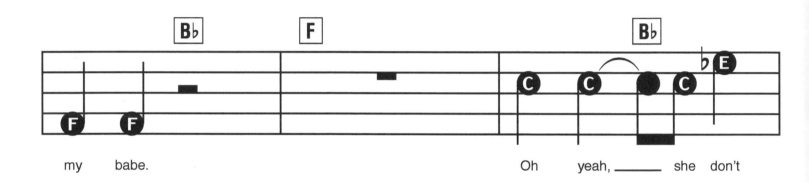

my babe. Oh yeah, _____ she don't

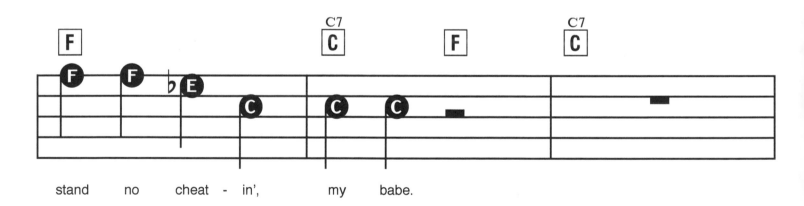

stand no cheat - in', my babe.

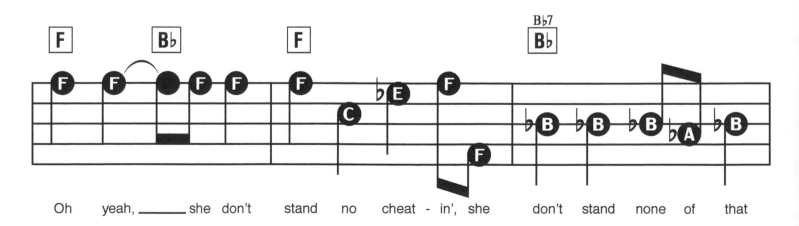

Oh yeah, _____ she don't stand no cheat - in', she don't stand none of that

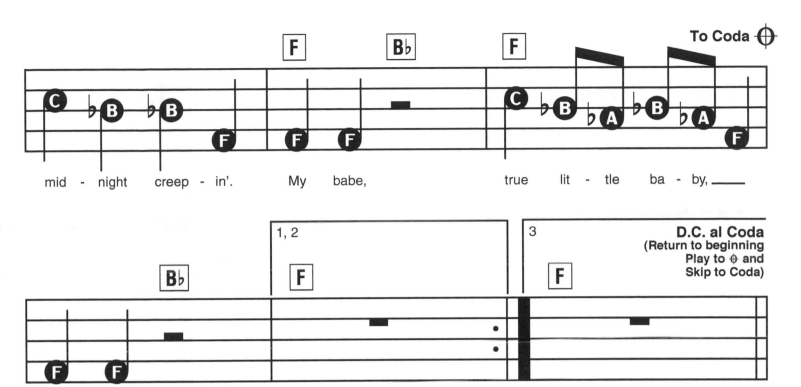

mid - night creep - in'.   My babe,   true lit - tle ba - by, ____

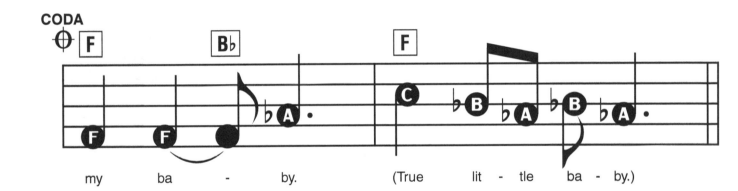

my   babe.

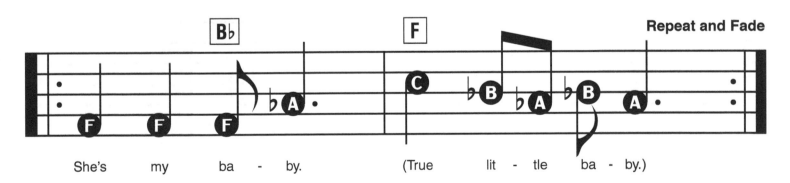

my   ba - by.   (True lit - tle ba - by.)

She's   my   ba - by.   (True lit - tle ba - by.)

Additional Lyrics

2. My babe, I know she love me, my babe.
   Whoa yes, I know she love me, my baby.
   Oh yes, I know she love me.
   She don't do nothing but kiss and hug me.
   My babe, true little baby, my babe.

3. My baby don't stand no cheatin', my babe.
   Oh no, she don't stand no cheatin', my baby.
   Oh no, she don't stand no cheatin'.
   Ev'rything she do, she do so pleasin'.
   My babe, true little baby, my baby.

4. My baby don't stand no foolin', my babe.
   Oh yeah, she don't stand no foolin', my baby.
   Oh yeah, she don't stand no foolin'.
   When she's hot, there ain't no coolin'.
   My babe, true little baby, my baby.

Night Train

Registration 8
Rhythm: Blues or Shuffle

Words by Oscar Washington and Lewis C. Simpkins
Music by Jimmy Forrest

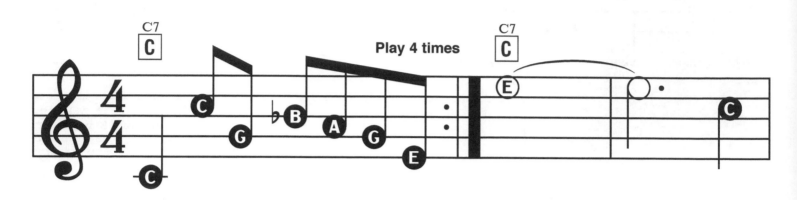

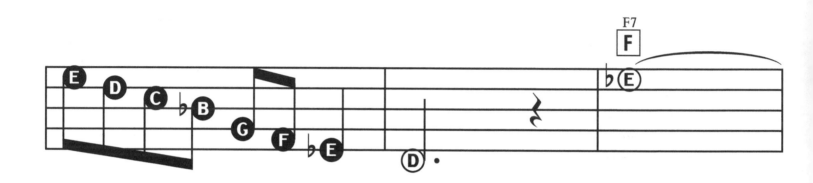

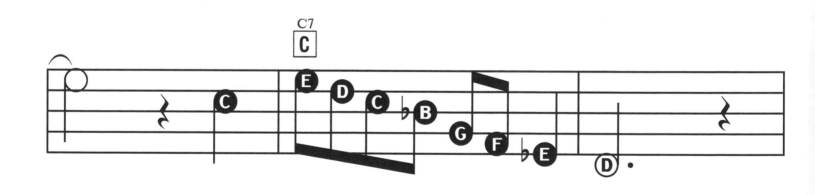

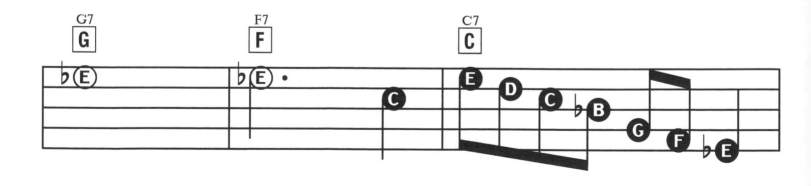

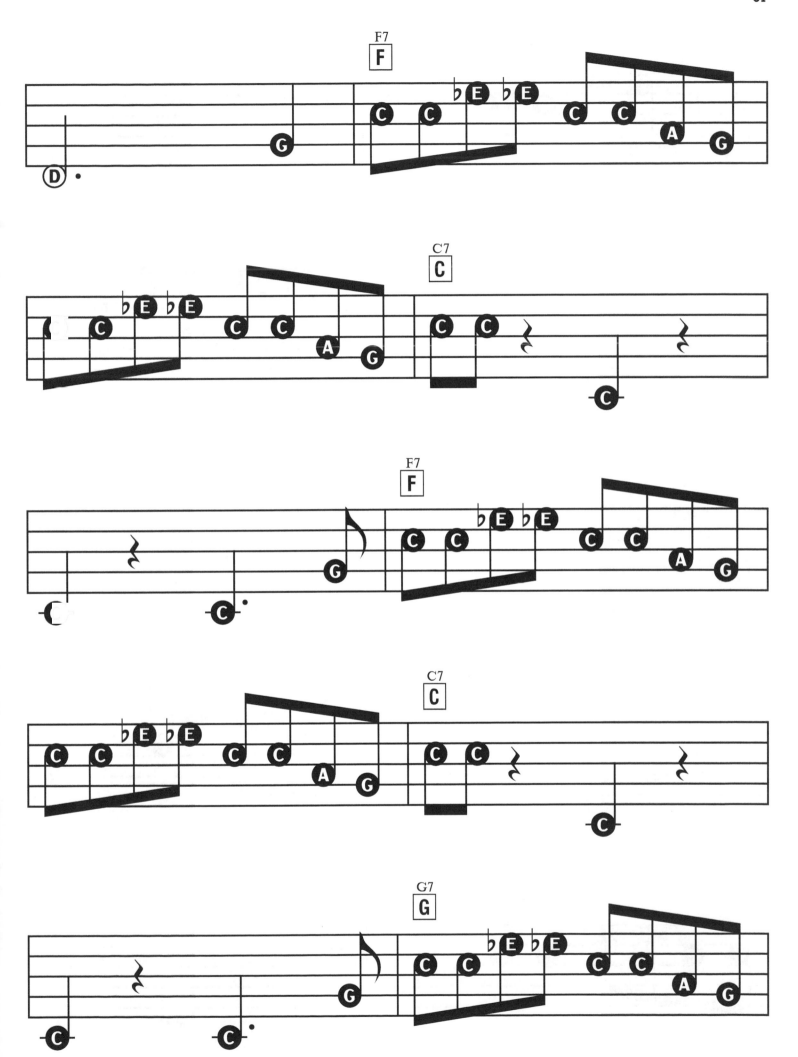

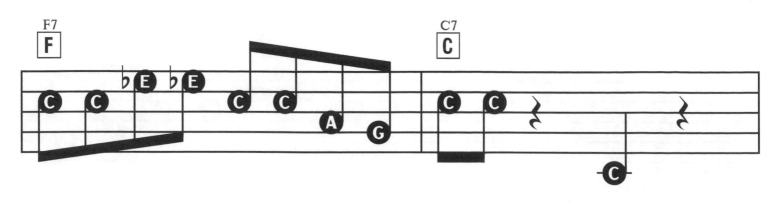

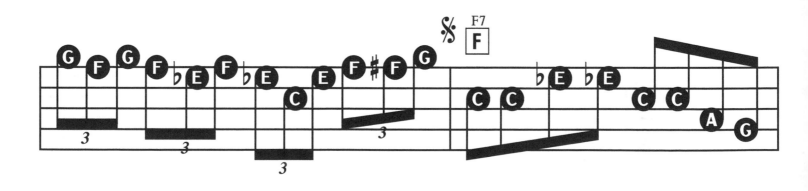

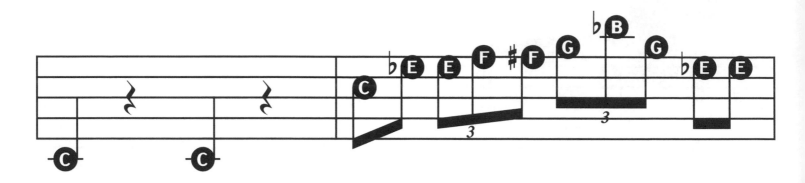

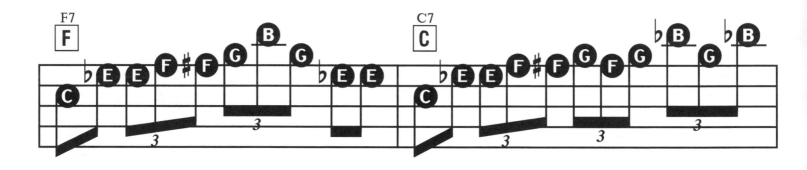

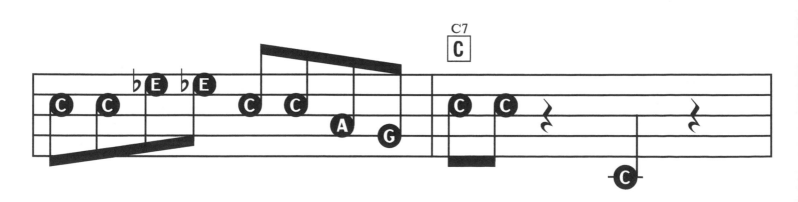

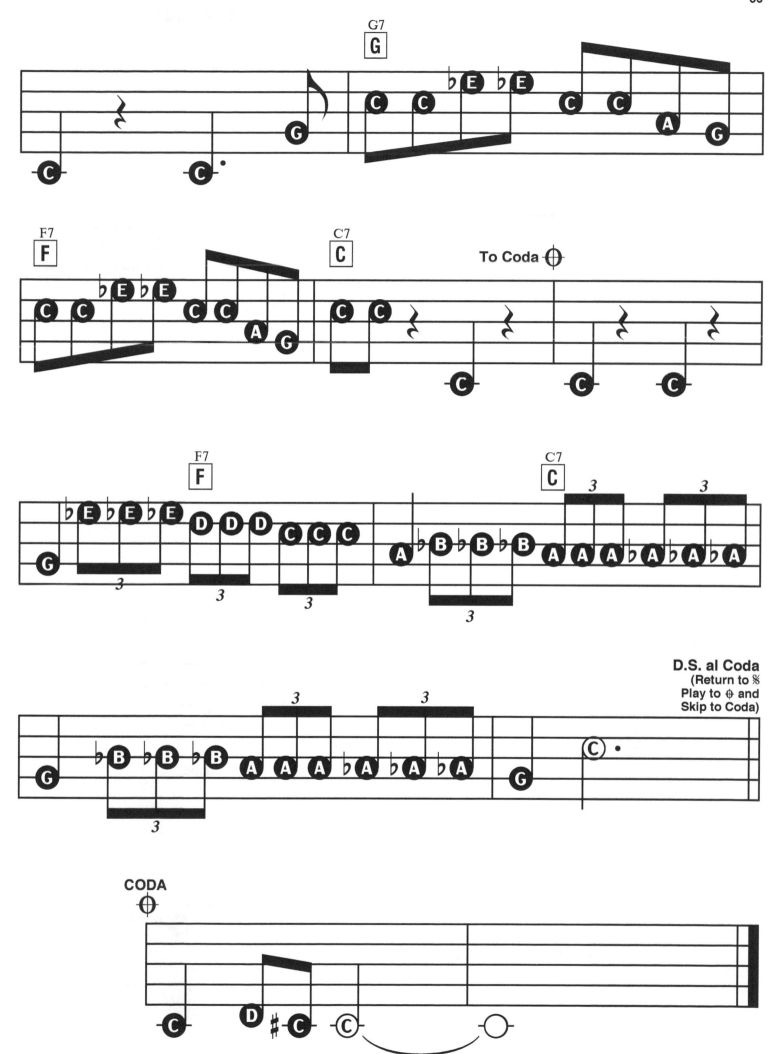

Nobody Knows You When You're Down and Out

Registration 8
Rhythm: Blues or Swing

Words and Music by
Jimmie Cox

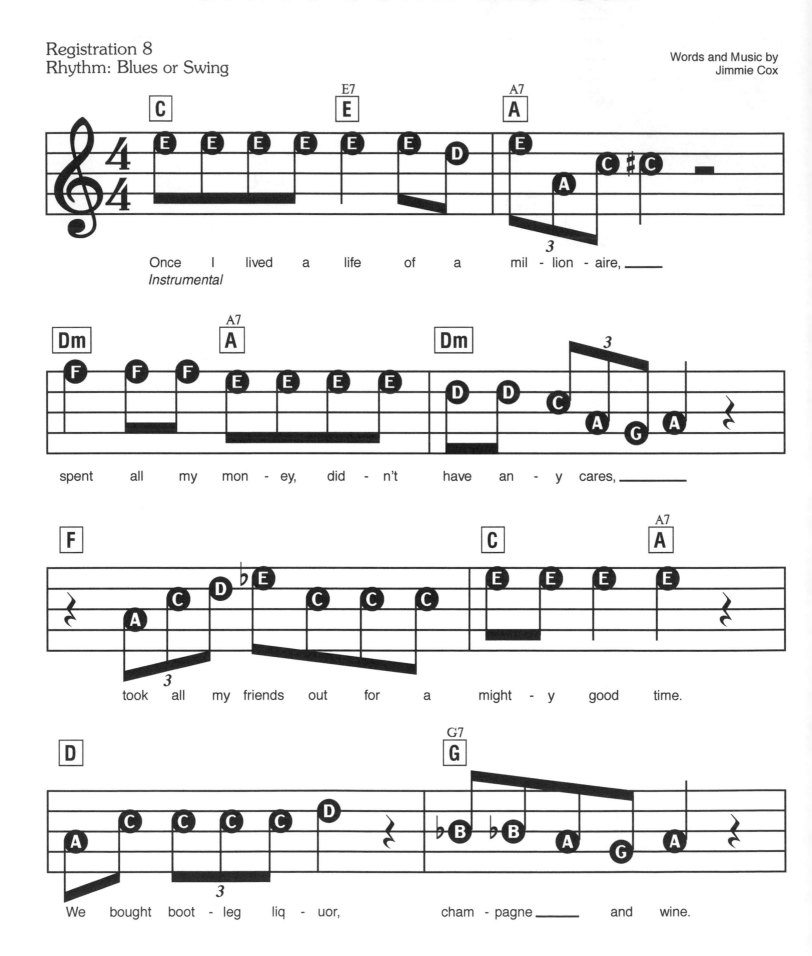

Once I lived a life of a mil - lion - aire, _____
Instrumental

spent all my mon - ey, did - n't have an - y cares, _____

took all my friends out for a might - y good time.

We bought boot - leg liq - uor, cham - pagne _____ and wine.

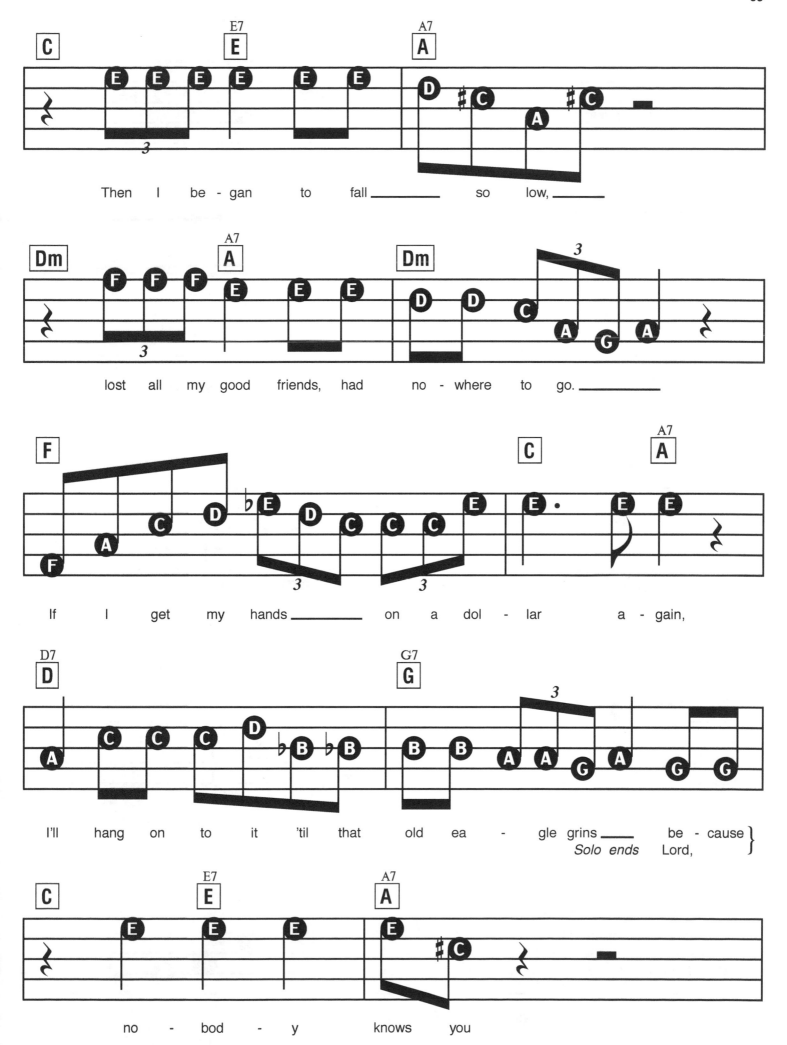

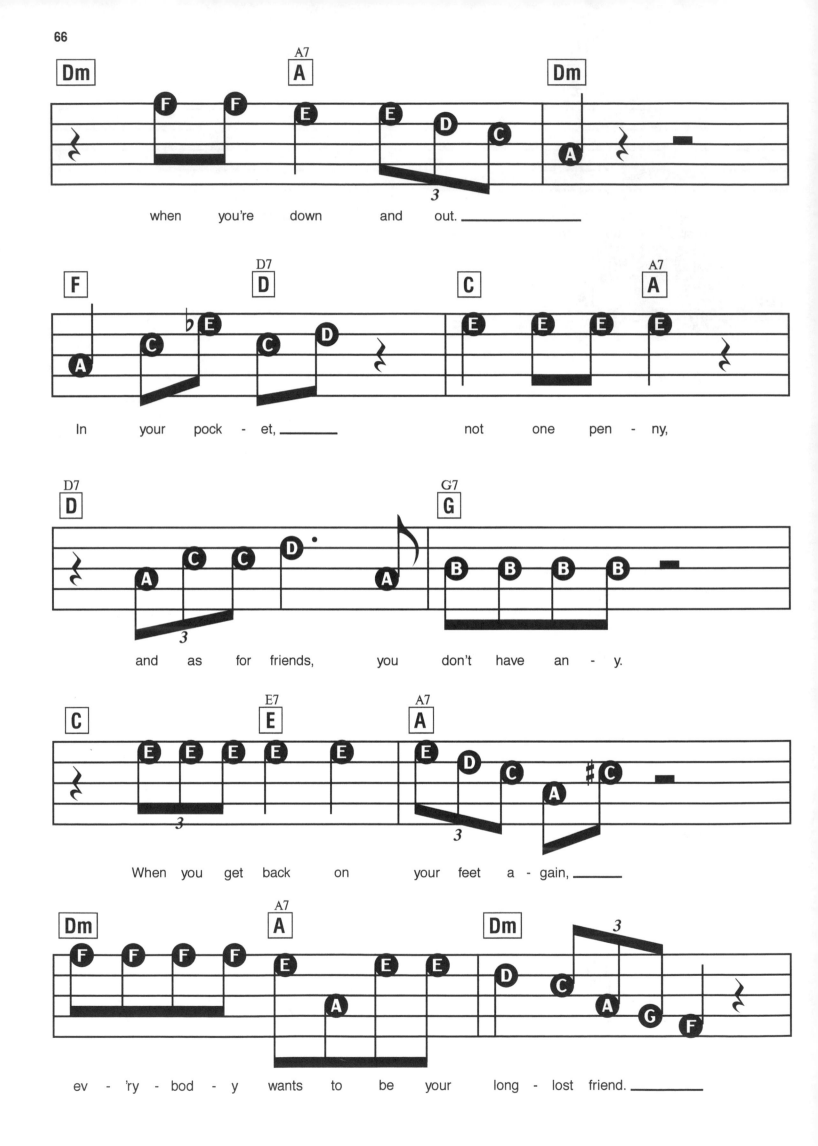

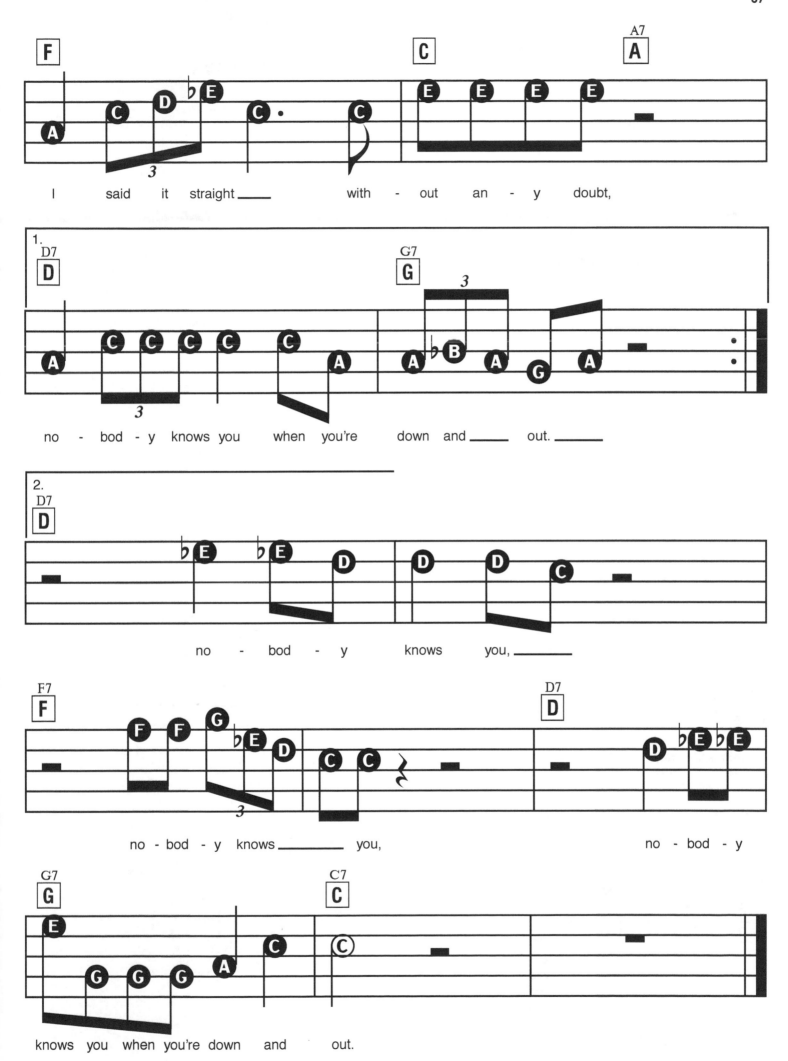

Stormy Weather
(Keeps Rainin' All the Time)
from COTTON CLUB PARADE OF 1933

Registration 2
Rhythm: Ballad or R&B

Lyric by Ted Koehler
Music by Harold Arlen

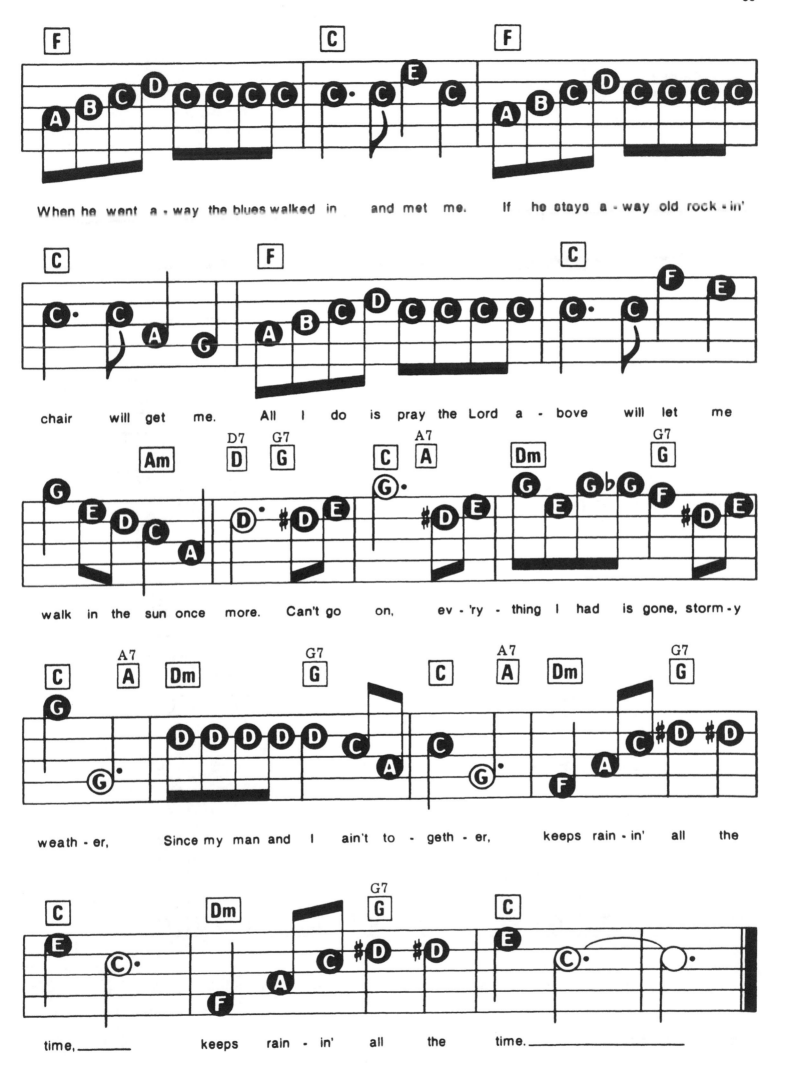

Route 66

Registration 7
Rhythm: Swing

By Bobby Troup

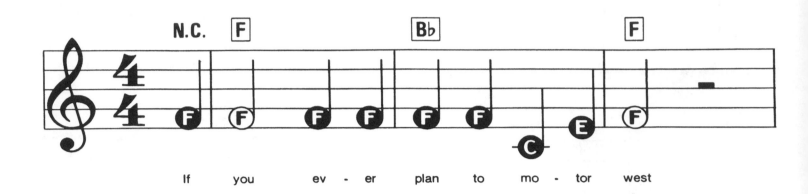

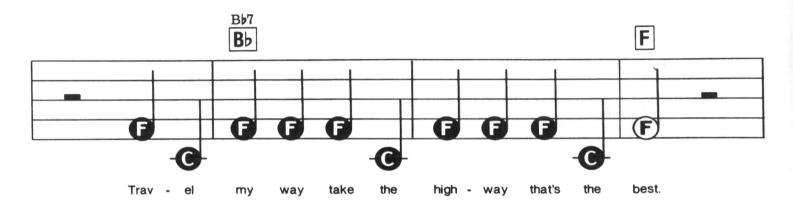

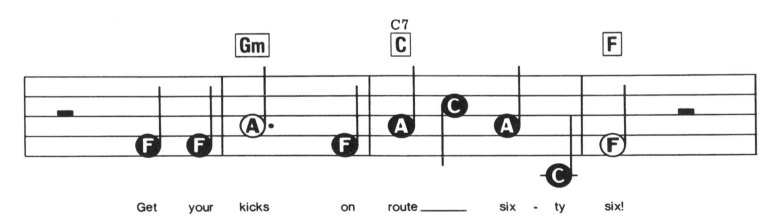

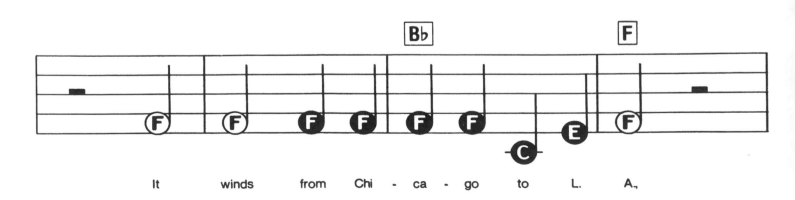

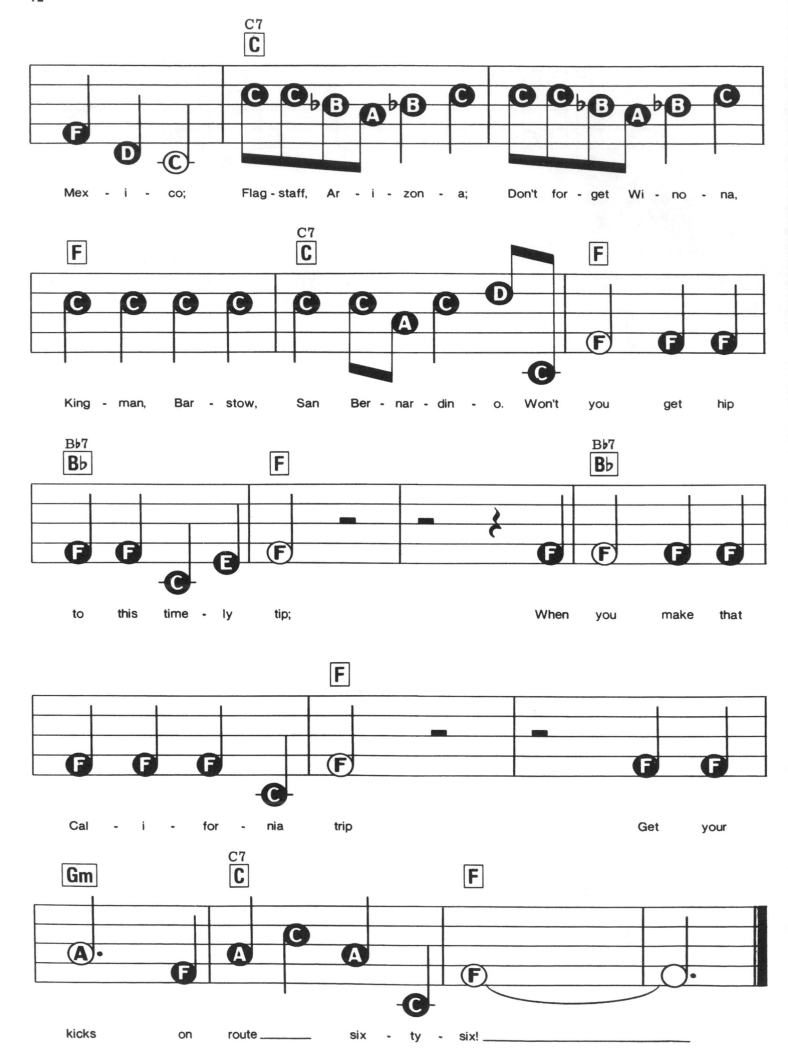